T0320270

Journalism, Online Comments, and the Future of Public Discourse

Comments on digital news stories and on social media play an increasingly important role in public discourse as more citizens communicate through online networks. The reasons for eliminating comments on news stories are plentiful. Off-topic posts and toxic commentary have been shown to undermine legitimate news reporting. Yet the proliferation of digital communication technology has revolutionized the setting for democratic participation. The digital exchange of ideas and opinions is now a vital component of the democratic landscape. Marie K. Shanahan's book argues that public digital discourse is a crucial component of modern democracy—one that journalists must stop treating with indifference or detachment—and for news organizations to use journalistic rigor and better design to add value to citizens' comments above the social layer. Through original interviews, anecdotes, field observations and summaries of research literature, Shanahan explains the obstacles of digital discourse as well as its promises for journalists in the digital age.

Marie K. Shanahan is an assistant professor of journalism at the University of Connecticut. Her teaching and academic research focus on the intersection of journalism and interactive communication technology. She has been a journalist, online news producer and professional writer for more than 20 years. Her interest in the possibilities of interactive media led her away from an early career as a print reporter at *The Hartford Courant* to the digital side of news, where she spent 13 years producing online news and dealing with comments on the web. Her academic work has been published by *The Poynter Institute*, *Columbia Journalism Review*, *The Chronicle of Higher Education*, *Newsweek*, *Salon* and *The Conversation*.

Journalism, Online Comments, and the Future of Public Discourse

Marie K. Shanahan

Routledge
Taylor & Francis Group

NEW YORK AND LONDON

First published 2018
by Routledge
711 Third Avenue, New York, NY 10017

and by Routledge
2 Park Square, Milton Park, Abingdon, Oxon OX14 4RN

Routledge is an imprint of the Taylor & Francis Group, an informa business

Library of Congress Cataloging-in-Publication Data
A catalog record for this book has been requested

ISBN: 978-1-138-63023-9 (hbk)
ISBN: 978-1-315-20957-9 (ebk)

Typeset in Times New Roman
by Apex CoVantage, LLC

Contents

Acknowledgments

Life is a collaborative process, and the generous collaboration of many teachers, colleagues, friends and family members enabled me to research and write this book.

For information and inspiration, I am grateful to my former colleagues in the newsroom at *The Hartford Courant*; my Quinnipiac University professors who introduced me to the complexities of interactive communications, particularly Alexander Halavais and Joseph H. Cooper; the fellows and faculty members from the 2015 Association of Opinion Journalists Minority Writers seminar; and the many hard-working journalists from the Online News Association, Society of Professional Journalists, Asian American Journalists Association and American Society of Journalists and Authors, who generously shared their knowledge and experiences with me.

For financial support, I was honored to receive a grant from the Public Discourse Project at the Humanities Institute at the University of Connecticut, with special thanks to director Michael P. Lynch.

For invaluable conversations, comments and editing, I am indebted to Kate Farrish, Maureen Croteau, Wayne Worcester, Marcel Dufresne, Lynne Delucia, Naedine Hazell, Donna Larcen, Helen Ubiñas, Jennifer Rancourt, my "Small Writers Group" writing buddies and each of my UConn Journalism colleagues.

For their limitless patience, love and support, I am forever thankful to my parents, siblings and cousins; my life partner, Todd; and my beautiful daughters, Julia and Ella.

Lastly, I extend sincere appreciation to all my current and former journalism students, whose fresh perspectives on digital discourse and online culture never fail to seed my curiosity.

1 Bystanders

For I take it that your silence gives consent.

—Plato, Cratylus, 435b[1]

On a late Friday afternoon in May 2008, a grandfather in Hartford, Connecticut, strolled out of a neighborhood grocery store with a bottle of milk tucked under his arm. As Angel Arce Torres stepped into the road to cross, a black Honda that was chasing after a tan Toyota swerved into the wrong lane, plowed into the 78-year-old and sped off without stopping. The impact sent the retired forklift operator's body flying onto the pavement, where he lay crumpled and bleeding.

The entire terrible scene was captured by a street surveillance camera. In seeking the public's help to identify the Honda's driver, the Hartford Police Department released a graphic 90-second recording of the crash to local news outlets. The disturbing video, enhanced by a state forensic science laboratory, immediately went viral. Not only did the footage show the depravity of the hit-and-run, it also seemed to show bystanders in one of Hartford's predominantly Hispanic neighborhoods ignoring the unconscious elderly man lying in the street. Nine cars and a motorcycle could be seen on the video driving past Torres's critically injured body while people on the sidewalk seem to do nothing until a police cruiser arrives about a minute and a half later.[2]

The perceived callousness displayed by bystanders on the video seized the public's attention more than the cruelty of the hit-and-run.[3] Intense local news coverage spread to morning radio talk shows and then to all the major national news outlets,[4] and online copies of the video were shared and viewed repeatedly on demand and out of context. A "heartless Hartford" narrative that the viral video supplied to detractors, accompanied by a remark from the police chief that the city had "lost its moral compass,"[5] provided the perfect recipe for what came next: the vicious online shaming of Connecticut's capital city and its residents.

Back in 2008, the go-to online forums for members of the public to post responses to news reports were slightly different than in 2017. Digital conversations about the news may now be commonplace on social media channels such as Facebook and Twitter, but in 2008, those networks had not yet reached critical mass. If a digital news consumer wanted to react to a story or opine on a topic to the widest possible audience, the best place to sound off was the same location where people read the news in the first place: the comment section at the bottom of the online news story.

My employer at the time—*The Hartford Courant*—offered the public just such a digital venue for venting. Any visitor to *Courant.com* could simply scroll to the end of any story to instantly and anonymously add their commentary to an open and always-on digital discussion space. Amid ongoing coverage of the hit-and-run, the *Courant's* anonymous, unmoderated online comment boards swelled with thousands of posts from around the country.

Extremes of emotion colored the comments. Some remarks were perceptive or heartfelt, but the majority of the discussion about the hit-and-run veered into racist, noxious and off-topic rhetoric about crime-ridden urban dwellers, Puerto Ricans and immigrants. The worst submissions disparaged the city's residents as "animals," "devils" and "barbarians" and described— ever so ironically—how Puerto Ricans, Hispanic immigrants and African Americans lacked "traditional New England standards of civility." Those comments, which can still be found online today,[6] labeled Hartford "an armpit," "scum," and so much worse.

The internet-fueled piling on reached a boiling point about three weeks later. On June 20, 2008, those of us working at the *Courant* found ourselves on the defensive when dozens of community activists, city officials and state representatives assembled on the *Courant's* doorstep to protest the newspaper's online comment sections.[7]

"These comments remain on the *Courant* website for hours, days—even months—after they have been posted, and attract similar types of comments," read a statement circulated by the Hartford mayor's office. "Hate speech has apparently been posted regularly on this website for many months without 'America's oldest continuously published newspaper' taking action."

The protest may have been the first time user comments published by a news organization *online* triggered an actual demonstration *offline*.

The protesters demanded that as a corporate citizen, the *Courant* should stop providing "a platform for hate and racist material."[8] They wanted the *Courant* to recognize its role in facilitating hate speech through its website, and apologize. They urged Connecticut's largest news organization to require commenters to register and post with real names attached, like old-fashioned letters to the editor. And they asked for a "community manager" to moderate online dialogue to prevent racist, violent and hateful posts from dominating comment sections.

As one of the digital journalists responsible for news content on the *Courant*'s website, I found the protesters' accusations mortifying but deserved. An insidious incivility had hijacked the *Courant's* comment sections, and we were confounded by the problem. The *Courant*, like the rest of the news industry, was already overwhelmed with the digital revolution upending the news business in the first decade of the 21st century. The news organization was preoccupied with how to reverse plummeting advertising revenue, shrinking subscriptions and newsrooms layoffs while somehow maintaining the core business of gathering and publishing the news. Dealing with online commenters and the Wild West culture that came with publishing on the World Wide Web was not a priority.

Adding to the comment problem was the *Courant*'s structurally flawed anonymous online commenting system, supplied by corporate parent Tribune Company. The glitches in that technology enabled unidentified perpetrators to exploit discussion spaces and commit nonstop digital hit-and-runs on the subjects of articles and the journalists reporting the stories. Since the *Courant* couldn't afford to devote limited staff to moderating user submissions, a laissez-faire comment moderation strategy allowed bigotry, threats of violence and libelous material to fester in user feedback areas like blighted neighborhoods, undermining the legitimate news content just a scroll above.

The *Courant*'s publisher at the time, Stephen D. Carver, responded to the protesters with a written statement denying that the newspaper intentionally promoted or fostered hate speech. He wrote that comments under news stories "are a reflection of a free society working at its best and at its worst."[9] The publisher drew a parallel between reader comment boards and Americans' First Amendment right to free speech: both were intrinsically valuable, if imperfect. Carver pledged the *Courant* would "certainly try to perfect the system as we go forward."

I found some agreement with my publisher's stance. *Some* of the online comments below *some* of the news stories were worthwhile. In the best cases, the *Courant*'s forums functioned as digital public squares for democratic deliberation, introducing ground-level voices and new, interesting vantage points to news stories. If journalism gains its power through connections to the audience, then comment areas could spur public (and paying customer) engagement. User submissions that were insightful, well informed or entertaining had the ability to enrich the original work of journalism, similar to how callers add texture to a radio talk show.[10]

But the dismay and the demands of the comment section critics in Hartford were legitimate, too. Here was their trusted Connecticut media institution not only supplying a stage for toxic commentary but also acting like an uninvolved bystander to the hate-filled digital assaults being perpetrated within its purview. Disregarding the discourse gave consent for a faceless, aggressive mob to set the tone.

Journalism's Comment Conundrum

> This was supposed to be the information age. Instead, we find ourselves in a swamp of rumor, innuendo and fake news.
>
> —Jeffrey Herbst, president & chief executive officer of the Newseum[11]

The Hartford Courant's comment quandary signaled—rather dramatically— how the news industry was failing to grapple with the disruption the internet had unleashed on the norms of public discourse. Journalism's complicated online comment problem served as the impetus for my academic research and the motivation for this book. Important ethical, legal and professional questions regarding the role of journalism in public digital discourse have only expanded since my experience at the *Courant*.

The internet enables and accelerates conversations in ways that were impossible in the previous era of mass media.[12] As a network of relationships, it is unmatched in its ability to facilitate public dialogue. Computer-mediated communication is eclipsing the conventional forms of public debate in the United States. It is easier for citizens to post comments online than to attend a town meeting or write a letter to the editor. Created on the paradigm of free-flowing discourse, the internet has inextricably altered the rules of human engagement.

The internet functions both as an intermediary and as a publishing device. Strangers who share interest in the same subjects, concerns or news topics— and who would never have met in person—can now find each other online, congregate and converse instantaneously, regardless of geographic location. Pervasive computer networking has freed people from analog constraints and boundaries like time and place, making human connection possible in a digital public sphere open to all.

Framed this way, digital discourse sounds radically utopian, in the same promising way Wikipedia founder Jimmy Wales once described his collaborative online encyclopedia as a "world in which every single person on the planet is given free access to the sum of all human knowledge."[13] But what journalists and the citizenry have come to experience in online discussions is nowhere near a nirvana of reliable information or reasoned public debate. Online public dialogue ranges from insightful musings to the foulest anonymous bile. For journalists, engaging the public in open digital feedback is to contend with variables that overworked, shrinking newsrooms did not foresee and were unprepared to handle. Rampant incivility, participation inequality, polarization, propaganda, distortion and distrust are among the digital discourse problems impinging upon the practices of journalism and its products. There is nothing that has engendered such a reputation for broken discourse as online comment sections.

Less than a quarter century ago, an average citizen seeking a substantial audience for an opinion had little choice but to work through a traditional media entity. The power to filter and reject or publish and promote salvos belonged to newspapers, magazines, radio and television stations. Those mainstream media outlets operate under professional codes of ethics and legal restrictions related to defamation, obscenity, indecency and copyright infringement. But digital self-publishing tools, social media and our new age of egalitarian information have dismantled the news media's role as society's information sieve.

By using the power of the internet, any person "can become a town crier with a voice that resonates farther than it could from any soapbox," wrote Justice John Paul Stevens in a 1997 U.S. Supreme Court decision.[14] Access to the internet gives all democratic actors in society—citizens, journalists, businesses, governments—an unparalleled means to engage directly in the exchange of information. What I refer to in this book as *public digital discourse* can be defined as the internet-powered virtual exchange of ideas and opinions between citizens in public view, with a focus on user comments on mainstream news websites and news-related social media posts.

Public comments appended to stories published by news sites have a greater chance of gaining high visibility.[15] Timely local and national news coverage is also more likely to stimulate public feedback. "The attractive part of online comments is the democratization of journalism. No longer does the published perception belong solely to the writer of the article. It belongs to whoever in the world has access to the internet," wrote Karen Klein, a free speech advocate and former *Los Angeles Times* editorial writer.[16]

Debugging the troublesome variables of public digital discourse, however, has been as exasperating for giant online platforms as it has been for hyperlocal news sites. The distribution democracy of the World Wide Web means everyone is now on the same network and angling for an audience. If the media has always been a game of attention,[17] then the open digital media landscape is an MMOG—a massively multiplayer online game whose prize is virality: shares, follows, comments, likes, as well as any ensuing outrage. News purveyors are just one competitor in this arena among millions of players seeking attention.

The following chapters will explore comments as the digital iteration of "conversation," examining how news-related public discussions function within a deliberative democracy and how journalism's challenge to "be a conversation rather than a lecture" in the digital age[18] is bedeviled by design defects and the obstacles of participatory online culture. Special attention will be given to the influence of anonymous online comments and journalism's contradictory relationship with anonymity.

There are strong forces contributing to journalism's bystander attitude toward comments. To make sense of what happened to forums on news sites is to recognize the collision of journalism, computer-mediated communication technology, comment system design, evolving audience information habits, political polarization and Section 230 of the Communications Decency Act of 1996. During my years working at the *Courant*, I saw the technological and financial constraints of my news organization, the lack of accountability provided by anonymity, and the inaction of news leaders allow the loudest, most prolific and most subversive members of the audience to take advantage of flaws in news comment boards with few or no repercussions.

The digital communication landscape is largely unbounded by the conventions that preceded it. News on the internet goes beyond mere consumption by the audience. The read-write web enables what computer science pioneers J.C.R. Licklider and Robert W. Taylor described as "cooperative modeling"—meaning cooperation in the construction, maintenance and use of a model with the public.

"We believe that communicators have to do something nontrivial with the information they send and receive . . . as active participants in an ongoing process, bringing something to it through our interaction with it," Licklider and Taylor explained. "A communication system should make a positive contribution to the discovery and arousal of interests."[19]

Two-way online engagement empowers the public's social commentary. The interactive onslaught of discourse has forced journalists to rethink how they gather and distribute news. Where once the business model of journalism was based on scarcity, it now involves organizing a deluge of data and public commentary that journalists did not play a role in creating.[20] Online comments also echo as a modern—albeit distorted—form of public opinion.[21] Digital exchanges that grab the attention of citizens and journalists have power to prompt, feed and/or advance news coverage.[22]

But an obvious schism hinders the "cooperative model" of digital news. Journalism, for the most part, is bound to professional standards and ethics. The audience is not. The resulting gap in the quality of digital discourse causes friction and conflict. For news organizations aiming to stimulate public debate, the merit of discussions anchored around online news stories is key to maintaining a credible community profile.[23] Comments from the audience create value for news organizations when they meet basic standards of journalism. Then that "value" can be confidently passed on to the larger news audience and amplified.

Commenters have organically brought value to the larger news audience through the distinct nature of their commentary, such as when they provide additional context to the news story that readers or viewers may have felt was lacking or through information updates on which additional stories can be built. Ideally, the comments section of a news story should be a marketplace of ideas, where users share anecdotes or counterpoints or pose unanswered questions. At the very least, user comments attached to works of journalism should address the topics highlighted in the respective story.

Journalists prefer informed opinions and varied perspectives that are civil, enlightening and/or entertaining. Journalists also favor user posts that introduce new information or reveal new sources for potential follow-up stories. It's the same kind of content a journalist seeks out when reporting a story. Commenters can disagree with the ideas presented in the news story and disagree strongly with the positions of other commenters, but the trouble ensues when commenters start to personally attack.

"It's 100% okay with us if you disagree with our opinions or want to point out something we've overlooked or think there's bias in an article. We rely on our commenters and community to holler if they see something amiss," wrote Engadget community content editor Amber Bouman when the tech news site took a hiatus from comments in March 2016. "There's really no point in a comments section where everyone agrees. But we are 100% not okay with insulting, demeaning, disrespectful, harassing or threatening behavior."[24]

Repeated exposure to vitriol can drive away the more level-headed members of the audience. Instead of fostering communication, a news site earns a reputation as a place for collective hissing, or a playground for trolls. Some commenters find visceral appeal in having potential access to the same sizeable audience as an influential local or national news organization. It takes just one or two unchecked bad actors or aggressive commenters with extreme views to fuel a general breakdown in civility and steer a forum into a negative "spiral of silence."[25] Research suggests that squabbling in comments sections turns off large segments of the public. A March 2016 survey by the Engaging News Project at the University of Texas at Austin found that slightly more than half of Americans don't read news comments or leave comments on news sites.[26]

So how can stressed newsrooms manage and capitalize on public digital discourse if the fire hose of user commentary contains misinformation, hate speech, libelous material and propaganda? When rude, hateful and harassing comments smother the contributions of civil audience members, the comment stream ceases to become useful. It turns into noise, or worse— destructive babel. "The sense of participatory collective—always fraught— has waned as more and more subcultures are crammed and collapsed into a common, traceable, searchable medium. We hang over each other's heads, more and more heavily, self-appointed *swords of Damocles* waiting with baited breath to strike," observed social media researcher Bonnie Stewart.[27]

Because people commonly utilize the internet as a social space, digital audiences are often encountering news while engaged in leisure. More than half of digital news consumers (55%) obtain news online while accomplishing other digital tasks, according to a 2016 Pew Research Center study.[28] Facebook, for example, provides a virtual venue for people to watch videos, shop, play games, community organize and share their opinions about anything and everything all at once. "What we're seeing is we just haven't found the right social signals or social codes to make people feel that they have to behave a certain way in certain spaces online—and to tell the difference between a club and a church," noted *Guardian* social and community editor Joanna Geary.[29]

The digital shift in the norms of public discourse has been unnerving for professional journalists who operated in a world before online comments. There are journalists and members of the public who view comments on news stories and on social media as a nuisance—even a civic menace.[30] Although the First Amendment provides legal protection for acrimonious remarks and hate speech, comments that are condescending, cruel, misogynistic, xenophobic and racist clash with journalistic ethics and choke meaningful debate.[31] While freedom of expression is a core principle upheld by journalists, the cringe-worthy online actions of trolls, terrorists and many ordinary citizens chip away at the meta-value of free speech and, consequently, of digital discourse.[32]

"[A]re we contributing to the reflexively cynical, hate-filled discourse that has polluted American civic life? Are we reviving the civic square? Or managing a sewer with toxic streams that demoralize anyone who dares to take part in government or citizen activism?"[33] These were questions *New Haven Independent* editor Paul Bass asked in 2012 after he paused the open forums on his local news site to reconsider whether the comments were doing more harm than good.

Lawrence B. Cook, a former journalist working as a Connecticut legislative press aide, expressed dismay with local newspapers and television stations that continue to allow online comments on their stories.

> Online comments are NOT generally comments about the specifics, pros and cons of the public policy issue at hand—they are merely opportunities for very angry and disaffected people to lash out, to re-state their prejudices, doubts and fears about everything and anything to anyone, regardless of the topic. The news story is just a springboard for their general animosity and ignorance. . . . I can only assume that media companies allow them because they contribute to page hits, which contribute

to higher online advertising revenues to make up for decreasing ad revenues. But in the bargain journalism is lost.[34]

Feedback Culture versus the "View from Nowhere"

> If you refuse to engage in the argument, you will lose the argument.
> —Jonathan Pie, the satirical UK News reporter
> persona of British actor Tom Walker[35]

As the internet has siphoned away the news media's authority as a gatekeeper of information, news organizations have compounded the digital discourse problem with ongoing neglect of their own leadership role as reliable conveners and moderators of public debate.

Online news producers at the *Hartford Courant* prior to 2008 were instructed to leave comment forums alone. The reasoning was three-fold. First, there was an overriding philosophy among news leaders that comment sections below stories were spaces belonging to readers. Let audience members use the forums under news content to talk among themselves. Second, refereeing arguments among readers was not the newsroom's responsibility. Journalists had more important jobs to do related to newsgathering and distribution. Third, thanks to Section 230 of the Communications Decency Act of 1996, online news publishers enjoy broad immunity regarding content created by users. Section 230 is considered the most important law protecting freedom of expression on the internet. It states, "No provider of an interactive computer service shall be treated as a publisher of any information provided by a third party."[36]

Section 230 enabled internet communication and digital commerce to flourish, but it also gave online publishers an excuse to ignore user-generated content on their sites. News sites are not liable for comments posted by users, even defamatory ones. Because of Section 230, comments under online news stories don't require the same labor-intensive vetting for falsities that printed letters to the editor or broadcast news stories demand. When news executives realized that editing comments might actually cause the news organization to become liable for what users posted, newsrooms cemented their hands-off-comments stance. Section 230's legal safeguards helped breed a newsroom culture of online comment neglect. Digital discourse on news sites couldn't help but devolve.

Calls to abandon comments have grown with journalists' anathema toward them. In 2013, shutting down on-site forums emerged as the quickest and easiest solution to the news industry's commenting woes. Online comments have been eliminated by a steady parade of news sites, most of which are now relying on Facebook and Twitter for interactions with the audience.

Popular Science most notably led the pack.[37] When the science publication ended comments, online content director Suzanne LaBarre defended the move by citing a research study that connected uncivil online comments with distortion in the public's perception of an issue.[38] "Comments sections tend to be a grotesque reflection of the media culture surrounding them," LaBarre explained. "Commenters shape public opinion; public opinion shapes public policy; public policy shapes how and whether and what [scientific] research gets funded—you start to see why we feel compelled to hit the 'off' switch."

"The conversation" once heralded as the future of journalism[39] is no longer present directly on digital news content published by National Public Radio,[40] Reuters,[41] The Daily Beast,[42] The Daily Dot,[43] The Week[44] and Mic,[45] to name a few.

Local television stations KOIN-TV in Seattle and WHSV-TV in Harrisonburg, Virginia, stopped commenting on online stories in January 2015.

"For every great, insightful comment or news tip I've seen over the past decade posted to the bottom of a story, I've dealt with 50 times more comments that add no value," wrote Tim Steele, KOIN's digital managing editor.[46]

In a WHSV.com note to the audience, the Virginia news station blamed a prolific group of eight or nine troublemakers for commandeering comments boards "to the extent that it is rare anyone else will leave comments."[47]

> Most of the users in violation of our policies have been banned from commenting more than once, but they change usernames or email addresses and return to continue their hate-mongering rhetoric as if they are in their own personal chat room. Rarely do these comments begin or end on anything associated with the story. Just one person among this group posted over 5,200 comments in the last 600 days. 166 of those comments were flagged for language alone.[48]

The editors of VICE were frank in justifying their prerogative to turn comments off in December 2016: "We don't have the time or desire to continue monitoring that crap moving forward."[49]

The *Missoulian* pulled the plug on comments in March 2017. "We have concluded that allowing comments on every story on our sites rarely adds consistent value to the public debate and, too often, hurts innocent subjects of the stories, makes the jobs of our reporters harder and harms the reputation of *The Missoulian*," explained Kathy Best, editor of the Montana news site. "The best use of our reporters and editors is to gather the news and act as watchdogs in our communities, not as bird dogs for online comments."[50]

When *The Berkshire Eagle* and its sister newspapers eliminated online commenting in September 2016, editor Kevin Moran announced the Pittsfield, Massachusetts-based news organization's decision to revert to a "tested, tried-and-true institution of communication": letters to the editor. "Larger media companies, like the *New York Times*, are able to employ a team of people to moderate reader comments to 'keep them on-topic and not abusive,' before they are published at the end of articles; it's a 24–7 job," Moran explained. "For smaller news outfits like us, that's just not practical. We had moderation controls on the online commenting tool dashboard, and while it filtered swear words just fine, it couldn't hold back nasty comments by people adept at sneaking past the syntax sentries."[51] Moran encouraged the audience to head over to social media to engage in conversations instead.

Thanks to social media networks, the digital frontier available for conversations about the news has expanded exponentially. Ways for users to engage in digital discourse keep broadening with mashup tools for images, audio, video and live streaming. Like a chicken-and-egg-argument, comment sections affixed to news content seem less necessary as news publishers have pushed audience engagement to Facebook and Twitter, and audiences spend more time on those social networks.

"We believe that social media is the new arena for commenting, replacing the old onsite approach that dates back many years," wrote Kara Swisher and Walt Mossberg on Re/Code's decision to end comments in 2014.[52]

Interestingly, as internet audiences have become *more active* in online conversations around news, a role reversal has taken place. Many news purveyors, understandably stunned by the avalanche of negative and inane online speech, have shrunk backward, *becoming passive* toward the idea of public digital discourse by either ignoring it (see popular mantra, "Don't read the comments"[53]) or by passing the buck to social networking sites.

Section 230 may legally absolve news sites that "don't read the comments," but allowing despicable missives to proliferate on news content makes journalists accomplices to the accumulating damage. There's a parallel in the H. G. Wells classic science fiction novel *The Invisible Man*. The morally challenged main character, Griffin, indicates his desire to establish a "reign of terror," but like a hostile online commenter, he can't get away with his bad behavior unless he has help from a complicit partner.

> I made a mistake, Kemp, a huge mistake, in carrying this thing through alone. I have wasted strength, time, opportunities. Alone—it is wonderful how little a man can do alone! To rob a little, to hurt a little, and there is the end. . . . What I want, Kemp, is a goal-keeper, a helper, and a hiding-place, an arrangement whereby I can sleep and eat and rest in

peace, and unsuspected. I must have a confederate. With a confederate, with food and rest—a thousand things are possible.[54]

As more members of the public gravitate to the web to discover and discuss the news of the day, the insolence of news-related discourse has not gone unnoticed by audience members, by the subjects of news stories or by the propagandists, spammers and trolls getting away with it. Social platforms do hold new opportunities for journalists to attract audiences since those networks have more users and higher rates of engagement. But social networks suffer the same public discourse problems of bullying, defamation and catch-as-catch-can moderation as news story comment sections, even more magnified. Online abuse can plague social media exchanges on a grand scale, attracting hundreds of thousands of participants and millions of lurkers. The #Gamergate controversy of 2014 and the vicious harassment of *Ghostbusters* actress Leslie Jones on Twitter in August 2016 are two examples of massive online abuse via social media.[55] Moderating discussions on social media is not any easier, either. Conversations in the coliseum of social media can spin out of control just as quickly. And the relentless sneer on social media is often the antithesis of a safe space for debate.[56]

"Social media platforms now edit and shape culture," observed NPR journalist Elise Hu, "even though they feel kind of allergic to that responsibility."[57]

Mainstream news sites, as independent online intermediaries themselves, have always had the freedom to configure standards for expression in their own spaces, but many have lacked the resources, knowledge or desire to do so. Revamping comment sections into constructive places that don't impede understanding or prevent consensus requires time and investment. Many local news organizations, unfortunately, don't have much of either to spare. "Talk is cheap, but dialogue comes at a considerable cost," noted *Chicago Magazine* digital editor Whet Moser.[58]

Journalists, however, cannot ignore this digital discourse problem any longer. Feedback culture is an unavoidable piece of journalism's future within the internet information ecosystem. The authors of *The Cluetrain Manifesto* accurately predicted in 1999 that the digital "conversation" around markets will happen and gain momentum, whether organizations are involved or not.[59] Audience feedback may be splintered and seething on social networks—particularly for news organizations that have eliminated on-site forums—but the conversation continues nonetheless.

In my view, news outlets undermine journalism's critical role in modern democracy—and their own viability—when they ignore the digital conversations prompted by their content, when they shut down the forums they control and when they pass responsibility for public discourse to third-party social media platforms.

"Uninvolved bystander" is the least ethical, strategic or prudent position for any professional news organization or journalist to take in the internet age. It's like a "view from nowhere"[60] approach to digital democratic discourse. If news organizations default to uninvolved bystander status in comment sections, they forfeit their ability to defend veracity, accountability, diversity and civility. They give away journalism's leadership role in a major setting for modern public democratic discourse.

If news companies and journalists don't prioritize interactive communication with their audiences or provide welcoming and productive places where their community members can talk with each other, the audience will organize itself and find other online feedback channels to engage, entertain themselves and call out uncomfortable truths. A hands-off approach to digital conversation pushes the market away and further diminishes journalism's role in our hyperconnected democratic society.

We've seen this happening already. There are influential members of the audience who have moved past news organizations to frame news topic narratives themselves in alternative online conversation spaces.[61] Political campaigns in particular have become sophisticated in the way they bypass media organizations to shape their own stories and cultivate their own audiences online. "If [companies] blow it, it could be their last chance," warned the authors of *The Cluetrain Manifesto*. "The community of discourse is the market. Companies that do not belong to a community of discourse will die."[62]

Notes

1. Plato. "Cratylus, 435b." *Plato in Twelve Volumes*. Vol. 12. Translated by Harold N. Fowler. Cambridge, MA: Harvard University Press; London: William Heinemann Ltd., 1921. Print.
2. User Googtubevideo. "Connecticut Hit and Run Victim Ignored." *YouTube Video*. 6 Jun. 2008. Web. www.youtube.com/watch?v=20BeOcjt52I
3. Angel Arce Torres died of his injuries one year later. He spent the remainder of his life in the hospital, paralyzed and on a respirator. The driver responsible for the hit-and-run was arrested one year later and prosecuted.
   Owens, David. "Park Street Hit-and-Run Victim Angel Arce Torres Dies." *Hartford Courant*. 12 May 2009. Web. www.courant.com/news/connecticut/hc-hc-hartford-park-street-0512.artmay12-story.html
   Petty, Lauren. "10 Years for Driver in Notorious Hit-and-Run." *NBC Connecticut*. 4 May 2010. Web. www.nbcconnecticut.com/news/local/Sentence-Comes-Today-in-Notorious-Hit-and-Run-92656219.html
4. "Gawkers Idle after Grisly Hit-and-Run." *Associated Press/CBS News*. 6 Jun. 2008. Web. www.cbsnews.com/news/gawkers-idle-after-grisly-hit-and-run/
5. Goren, Daniel E., and Mark Spencer. "City's Glaring Reflection: Police Chief's Harsh Words Spark Examination of Hartford's Heart, Soul and Character."

Hartford Courant. 6 Jun. 2008. Web. www.courant.com/news/connecticut/hc-parkstreethitrun-0608-story.html

A year later, Hartford Police Chief Daryl Roberts said he had changed his opinion of the city after the driver, Luis Negron, was arrested in May 2009. Roberts said he believed Hartford was a caring community because people came forward with information leading to Negron's arrest on the same day as Angel Arce Torres's funeral. See "Guilty Plea Ends Shocking Hit-and-Run Case." *Associated Press via CBS News*. 22 Feb. 2010. Web. www.cbsnews.com/news/guilty-plea-ends-shocking-hit-and-run-case/

6. Topix comment boards from 2008 are archived online. Multiple copies of the same discussion threads can be found under different Topix web addresses. Although comment boards could be hidden from view on the *Hartford Courant*'s website, they could still be found open and active on the websites of the *Orlando Sentinel*, *Chicago Tribune* or main Topix site. *The Courant* no longer uses Topix as its commenting system.

7. Cohen, Jeffrey B., and Daniel E. Goren. "Perez Confronts the Courant: Mayor Holds Protest at Newspaper's Headquarters against Hate Speech on Website." *Hartford Courant*. 21 Jun. 2008. Web. http://articles.courant.com/2008-06-21/news/perez0621.art_1_perez-free-speech-comments

8. Puleo, Tom. "Mayor Slams Paper's Forum, Calls Website a Platform for Hate Speech, Racism." *Hartford Courant*. 17 Jun. 2008. Web. http://articles.courant.com/2008-06-17/news/cttopix0617.art_1_discussion-forums-comments-boards

9. Cohen and Goren. "Perez Confronts the Courant."

10. Shanahan, Marie K. "How Talk Radio Listens to Its Audience, Provides Lessons for Online Publishers." *The Poynter Institute*. 4 Mar. 2014. Web. www.poynter.org/2014/how-talk-radio-listens-to-its-audience-provides-lessons-for-online-publishers/241945/

11. Herbst, Jeffrey. "How to Beat the Scourge of Fake News." *Wall Street Journal Opinion*. 11 Dec. 2016. Web. www.wsj.com/articles/how-to-beat-the-scourge-of-fake-news-1481491264

12. Levine, Rick, Christopher Locke, Doc Searls, and David Weinberger. *The Cluetrain Manifesto*. 10th Anniversary Paperback Edition. New York: Basic Books, 2011. XIV. Print.

13. Wales, Jimmy. "The Birth of Wikipedia." *TEDGlobal*. Oxford, UK. Jul. 2005. TED.com. Web. www.ted.com/talks/jimmy_wales_on_the_birth_of_wikipedia/transcript?language=en

14. Reno v. American Civil Liberties Union, 521 US 844—Supreme Court 1997, was the first major Supreme Court ruling on the regulation of materials distributed via the internet. Full text of the judgment is available at www.law.cornell.edu/supct/html/96-511.ZS.html

15. Nagar, Na'ama. "The Loud Public: The Case of User Comments in Online News Media." Order No. 3460834 State University of New York at Albany. Ann Arbor: ProQuest, 2011. Web. http://search.proquest.com/docview/879043165

16. Klein, Karin. "The Sacramento Bee Test: Is It Possible to Comment Civilly Online?" *Los Angeles Times Opinion*. 26 Nov. 2013. Web. www.latimes.com/opinion/opinion-la/la-ol-sacramento-bee-online-comments-20131126-story.html#ixzz2lqxtDDWR

17. Malik, Om. "The Distribution Democracy and the Future of Media." *Gigaom*. 10 May 2011. Web. https://gigaom.com/2011/05/10/the-distribution-democracy-and-the-future-of-media

18. Gillmor, Dan. "We the Media: The Rise of Citizen Journalists." *National Civic Review*. Fall 2004. Volume 93, Issue 3. Web. http://dx.doi.org/10.1002/ncr.62

19. Licklider, J.C.R., and Robert W. Taylor, "The Computer as a Communication Device." *Science and Technology* (1968). Print.

20. Little, Mark. "Writing a New Rulebook for Journalism." *Storyful*. 30 Oct. 2014. Web. https://storyful.com/blog/2014/10/30/harnessing-the-power-of-social-media-in-modern-journalism/

21. Friemel, T. N., and M. Dötsch. "Online Reader Comments as Indicator for Perceived Public Opinion." In M. Emmer and C. Strippel (Hrsg.), *Kommunikationspolitik für die digitale Gesellschaft*. 2015. Web. http://dx.doi.org/10.17174/dcr.v1.8

22. Herrman, John. "Self-Correcting beyond a Web Era Marked by Sensationalism." *New York Times*. 20 Mar. 2016. Web. www.nytimes.com/2016/03/21/business/media/self-correcting-beyond-a-web-era-of-sensationalism.html?_r=0

23. Diakopoulos, Nicholas, and Naaman Mor. "Towards Quality Discourse in Online News Comments." *Proceedings of the ACM 2011*. Conference on Computer-Supported Cooperative Work. 2011. Web. http://dx.doi.org/10.1145/1958824.1958844

24. Bouman, Amber. "We're Shutting Down Our Comments." *Engadget*. 25 Mar. 2016. Web. www.engadget.com/2016/03/25/were-shutting-down-our-comments-see-you-next-week/

25. Hampton, Keith, Lee Rainie, Weixu Lu, Maria Dwyer, Inyoung Shin, and Kristen Purcell. "Main Analysis: Political Issues and the Spiral of Silence." *Pew ResearchCenter*. Internet, Science & Tech. 26 Aug. 2014. Web. www.pewinternet.org/2014/08/26/main-analysis-political-issues-and-the-spiral-of-silence/

26. Stroud, Natalie (Talia) Jomini, Emily Van Duyn, and Cynthia Peacock. "Survey of Commenters and Comment Readers." *Engaging News Project*. 14 Mar. 2016. Web. https://engagingnewsproject.org/research/survey-of-commenters-and-comment-readers/

27. Stewart, Bonnie. "Something Is Rotten in the State of… Twitter." *Personal Blog*. 2 Sept. 2014. Web. http://theory.cribchronicles.com/2014/09/02/something-is-rotten-in-the-state-of-twitter/

28. Mitchell, Amy, Jeffrey Gottfried, Michael Barthel, and Elisa Shearer. "How Americans Get Their News: Pathways to News." *Pew Research Center Journalism Project*. 7 Jul. 2016. Web. www.journalism.org/2016/07/07/pathways-to-news/

29. O'Donovan, Caroline. "Q&A: Guardian Social and Community Editor Joanna Geary Heads off to Twitter U.K." *Nieman Lab*. 1 Oct. 2013. Web. www.niemanlab.org/2013/10/qa-guardian-social-and-community-editor-joanna-geary-heads-off-to-twitter-u-k/

30. Citron, Danielle Keats. "Free Speech Does Not Protect Cyberharassment." *New York Times*. 14 Aug. 2014. Web. www.nytimes.com/roomfordebate/2014/08/19/the-war-against-online-trolls/free-speech-does-not-protect-cyberharassment

31. Grimm, Fred. "The Year Lies, Insults, Threats and Fat Shaming Supplanted Civil Discourse." *Miami Herald*. 30 Dec. 2016. Web. www.miamiherald.com/news/local/news-columns-blogs/fred-grimm/article123664969.html

32. Shanahan, Marie K. "Media: Radical Shift in Control of the News." *Hartford Courant*. 19 Oct. 2014. Web. www.courant.com/courant-250/your-moments/hc-courant-future-media-20141018-story.html

33. Bass, Paul. "Time Out!" *New Haven Independent*. 8 Feb. 2012. Web. www.newhavenindependent.org/index.php/archives/entry/time_out/

34. Cook, Lawrence B. Email interview. 14 Oct. 2015.
35. Pie, Jonathan. "What's That Coming over the Hill? It's the Tories! JP Reacts to the Brexit Fallout and Slags off the Left for Once." [VIDEO]. 3 Jul. 2016. Web. www.facebook.com/JonathanPieReporter/videos/936993456423548/
36. "47 U.S. Code § 230: Protection for Private Blocking and Screening of Offensive Material." *Legal Information Institute*. Cornell Law School. Web. www.law.cornell.edu/uscode/text/47/230
37. LaBarre, Suzanne. "Why We're Shutting Off Our Comments." *Popular Science*. 24 Sept. 2013. Web. www.popsci.com/science/article/2013-09/why-were-shutting-our-comments
38. Anderson, Ashley A., Dominique Brossard, Dietram A. Scheufele, Michael A. Xenos, and Peter Ladwig. "The 'Nasty Effect': Online Incivility and Risk Perceptions of Emerging Technologies." *Journal of Computer-Mediated Communication*. Apr. 2014. Volume 19, Issue 3. 373–87. Web. http://onlinelibrary.wiley.com/doi/10.1111/jcc4.12009/full
39. Marchionni, Doreen. "Big Idea: Conversational Journalism." *The Poynter Institute*. 23 Jul. 2009. Web. www.poynter.org/2009/big-idea-conversational-journalism/97407
40. Montgomery, Scott. "Beyond Comments: Finding Better Ways to Connect with You." *NPR*. 17 Aug. 2016. Web. www.npr.org/sections/npr-extra/2016/08/17/490208179/beyond-comments-finding-better-ways-to-connect-with-you
41. "Editor's Note: Reader Comments in the Age of Social Media." *Reuters*. 7 Nov. 2014. Web. http://blogs.reuters.com/great-debate/2014/11/07/editors-note-reader-comments-in-the-age-of-social-media
42. "A Note to Our Readers." *The Daily Beast*. 19 Oct. 2015. Web. www.thedailybeast.com/articles/2015/08/19/a-note-to-our-readers.html
43. Powell, Austin, and Nicholas White. "Why We're Killing Our Comments Section." *The Daily Dot*. 27 Jul. 2015. Web. www.dailydot.com/company/comments-section-dead/
44. Frumin, Ben. "Why TheWeek.com Is Closing the Comments Section." *The Week*. 15 Dec. 2014. Web. http://theweek.com/articles/441774/why-theweekcom-closing-comments-section
45. "A Note to Our Readers about Commenting." *Mic*. 16 Oct. 2015. Web. https://mic.com/articles/106656/a-note-to-our-readers-about-commenting#.y8nYc5Gim
46. Steele, Tim. "Why KOIN.com Turned off Our Comment Boards." *KOIN.com*. 28 Jan. 2015. Web. http://koin.com/2015/01/28/why-koin-com-turned-off-our-comment-boards.
    Also, Stabler, David. "Fed Up, KOIN TV Turns off Comment Boards on Online News Stories." *OregonLive.com*. 29 Jan. 2015. Web. www.oregonlive.com/portland/index.ssf/2015/01/fed_up_koin_tv_turns_off_comme.html
47. "Changes to the WHSV Website." *WHSV.com*. 5 Jan. 2015. Web. www.whsv.com/home/headlines/Changes-to-the-WHSV-Website-287544861.html
48. Ibid.
49. Smith, Jonathan. "We're Getting Rid of Comments on VICE.com." *VICE*. 20 Dec. 2016. Web. www.vice.com/en_us/article/were-getting-rid-of-comments-on-vice
50. Best, Kathy. "Pulling the Plug on Online Comments." *Missoulian.com*. 6 Mar. 2017. Web. http://missoulian.com/pulling-the-plug-on-online-comments/article_6bf313cb-c53c-5d14-b10f-84f5506ff013.html
51. Moran, Kevin. "Eagle Bids Farewell to Online Comments." *The Berkshire Eagle*. 23 Sept. 2016. Web. www.berkshireeagle.com/stories/eagle-bids-farewell-to-online-comments,164141

52. Swisher, Kara, and Walt Mossberg. "A Note to Re/code Readers." *Re/code*. 20 Nov. 2014. Web. www.recode.net/2014/11/20/11633104/a-note-to-recode-readers

53. Valenti, Jessica. "Not All Comments Are Created Equal: The Case for Ending Online Comments." *The Guardian*. 10 Sept. 2015. Web. www.theguardian.com/commentisfree/2015/sep/10/end-online-comments

54. Wells, H. G. "Chapters XXIV: The Plan That Failed." *The Invisible Man: A Grotesque Romance*. Project Gutenberg, 7 Oct. 2004. Web. www.gutenberg.org/files/5230/5230-h/5230-h.htm

55. VanDerWerff, Todd. "Why Is Everybody in the Video Game World Fighting? #Gamergate." *Vox*. 6 Sept. 2014. Web. www.vox.com/2014/9/6/6111065/gamergate-explained-everybody-fighting.

   Also, Silman, Anna. "A Timeline of Leslie Jones's Horrific Online Abuse." *New York Magazine*. 24 Aug. 2016. Web. http://nymag.com/thecut/2016/08/a-timeline-of-leslie-joness-horrific-online-abuse.html

56. Shanahan, Marie K. "Yes, Campuses Should Be Safe Spaces—for Debate." *The Chronicle of Higher Education*. 31 Jan. 2016. Web. www.chronicle.com/article/Yes-Campuses-Should-Be-Safe/235114

57. Hu, Elise. "Silicon Valley's Power over the Free Press: Why It Matters." *NPR*. 24 Nov. 2014. Web. http://n.pr/1Cg4HLG

58. Moser, Whet. "Making Internet Comments Sound Smart Isn't Easy or Cheap." *Chicago Magazine*. 16 Apr. 2014. Web. www.chicagomag.com/city-life/April-2014/Turning-Internet-Comments-into-Dialogue-Isnt-Easy-or-Cheap/

59. Levine, Locke, Searls, and Weinberger. *The Cluetrain Manifesto*.

60. Rosen, Jay. "The View from Nowhere: Questions and Answers." *PressThink*. 10 Nov. 2010. Web. http://pressthink.org/2010/11/the-view-from-nowhere-questions-and-answers

61. Lewis, Hilary. "Derek Jeter Teams with Legendary to Launch the Players' Tribune." *The Hollywood Reporter*. 1 Oct. 2014. Web. www.hollywoodreporter.com/news/derek-jeter-teams-legendary-launch-737142

   Also, Altimari, Daniela. "In U.S. Senate Race, McMahon and Murphy Sticking to Prepared Scripts." *The Hartford Courant*. 23 Oct. 2012. Web. www.courant.com/news/elections/hc-sen-scripted-campaign-20121023-story.html

62. Levine, Locke, Searls, and Weinberger. *The Cluetrain Manifesto*.

2   A Story Is a Promise
of a Conversation

We want to be a part of elevating the conversation as opposed to being a part of the firestorm.
> —Katie Vogel, engagement editor at *The Cincinnati Enquirer*[1]

In the computer software development industry, there is a popular project management approach known as "Agile." It helps programmers as they build and refine software to emphasize collaboration and continual learning. One of the most dependable tools Agile teams rely upon to combat the confusion of large-scale projects is the "user story."[2] Programmers collect the perspectives of end-users in "stories"—short summaries of what users want from the software and why. The user stories make Agile developers more aware of important functional elements for the software before it's complete, affording them the opportunity to incrementally improve it. The purpose of a user story in Agile is to encourage collaboration. It is a "promise to have a future conversation."[3]

A parallel can be drawn from Agile user stories to the online comments posted on news story forums. Both function as "talking points," a "to-do list," or a "tickler that a conversation must occur."[4] Like software development, newsgathering is an iterative process, never more so than in the breakneck 24/7 news cycle of the digital age. News stories don't have tidy endings. The nature of news is incremental with updates, reaction and fallout. News creation is dependent upon collaboration with members of the public. Timely and relevant online comments can signal audience interest in a topic and suggest whether additional or revised news coverage is needed.

Journalists have come to expect engaged audience members to "talk back" to them about the products of their labor, especially if the news content is insightful, provocative, opinionated, emotional or erroneous. Political scientist Bernard C. Cohen's classic summation of the agenda-setting function of the mass media supports the conversation-starting by-product of news. "The press is significantly more than a purveyor of information and opinion," Cohen wrote in 1963.[5] "It may not be successful much of the time in telling people what to think, but it is stunningly successful in telling its readers what to think about."

News consumers in the digital age aren't confined to merely thinking about the issues raised in news reports. Empowered by read-write internet connectivity, they too are "users" who can react, respond, organize into groups and publish their own stories about what they want and why. "The easy possibility of communicating effectively into the public sphere allows individuals to reorient themselves from passive readers and listeners to potential speakers and participants in a conversation," explained information technology researcher Yochai Benkler about the emergence of a networked public. "The network allows all citizens to change their relationship to the public sphere. They no longer need to be consumers and passive spectators. They can become creators and primary subjects. It is in this sense that the Internet democratizes."[6]

As of 2016, more than 3.5 billion people are connected to the internet—that's 47% of the world's population armed with the potential to exchange news, knowledge, culture and opinions through digitally networked devices.[7] Participation can happen anytime and anywhere, revolutionizing the dimensions for private and public conversations stimulated by news reports.

For news purveyors, the foundation of audience engagement is conversation.[8] Information posted by audience members in comment forums can be considered a digital iteration of conversation. Conversation is also "the soul of democracy."[9] Political theorists contend it is through conversation—discussions both formal and informal—that citizens "bridge their personal experiences with the political worlds out there."[10] "The most fundamental and most ubiquitous democratic practice," observed media effects researcher Peter Dahlgren, "is civic interaction and discussion."[11]

The Public Sphere and Public Opinion

> A journalist's job, at its very essence, is to explain to the public what's going on. If the public is learning that through comments, journalists must be part of that discussion.
>
> —Gina Masullo Chen[12]

Journalism has long existed in the service of informed democracy. As defined by Bill Kovach and Tom Rosenstiel in their seminal book *The Elements of Journalism*, journalism is the activity of gathering, assessing, creating and presenting news and information.[13] Professional journalism is also the product of these activities—the news content delivered via newspapers, television, radio and the internet assembled by paid, trained and supervised journalists who work within established editorial norms. The fundamental purpose of journalism is to provide people with verified information they can use to make better decisions. The job of the journalist centers on clarifying complicated issues for the general public, which helps informed citizens make their democratic choices.

Like other forms of media, journalism subsists and thrives on an attention economy. Journalists aim to make "the significant" interesting and relevant by presenting information in such a way that people will be inclined to listen.[14] Whether news is printed, broadcast or distributed online, journalism becomes most effective when it prompts public awareness, inspires reflection and spurs dialogue. News reports that capture the right kind of attention gain some agenda-setting influence through the ability to provoke sustained public debate. By building traction for "common conversations" about the important topics that people may be reluctant to acknowledge or that are difficult to understand, news stories can be the catalyst for larger public discussions at the local, national and international levels.[15]

Citizen-to-citizen deliberation in the public sphere has the power to generate and mobilize public opinion, which in turn can shape the policies of the state and the development of society as a whole.[16] In a democracy, the force of public opinion expressed in the public sphere exerts pressure on elected or appointed officials.

Online comment forums can be considered a modern (and imperfect) version of the "public sphere." The common definition of public sphere originates with German sociologist and philosopher Jürgen Habermas, who conceived it as a central arena for societal communication where the citizenry expresses opinions, debates problems of general concern and develops collective solutions.[17] The concept of the public sphere emerged in the 18th century from the informal citizen gatherings in town squares, coffee houses and salons, where free and open arguments were made about any issues affecting citizens, without respect to rank or privilege. The English term "public sphere" comes from the German word *Öffentlichkeit*, which translates into two related terms—"the public" or the collective of speakers and listeners present, and "publicness" or the state of being visible and subject to scrutiny by the public.[18]

The mass media, and now digital media, support and sustain communication in the public sphere.[19] The internet integrates dimensions of the public sphere when cyberspace serves as a venue where citizens gather and engage in conversations. In his book *The Internet in China: Cyberspace and Civil Society*, Zixue Tai explains how the internet has not only enhanced the interactivity of conventional media forms but also fostered brand new types of "social spaces."[20] Tai's ideas build upon the community organizing ideas of urban sociologist Ray Oldenburg, who ranked human social environments.[21] Oldenburg contends the most important "first place" in a community is the home. The places where we work are our "second place" since work is required and serious and "reduces the individual to a single productive role." Our "third place" is composed of those informal, neutral, public social spaces we visit voluntarily—where "conversation is the primary activity and the main vehicle for the display and appreciation of human personality and individuality." Our social interactions in restaurants and coffee shops can resemble a home away from home, Oldenburg points out, because they are familiar and welcoming and offer psychological comfort and support. The third place also upholds a crucial role in quality community life as part of the public sphere. The First Amendment freedoms of association and assembly are at the heart of third places and essential to the democratic political process, Oldenburg explains.[22]

Tai proposes that the internet and its many online communities constitute a distinct "fourth place" for human interaction. The internet "marks a dramatic departure from all previous communication models," and its "transformative power lies in its ability to act as a social space where people gather, interact, gossip, banter, play games and do many, many more things that groups do," Tai argues.[23] Online gathering places such as Facebook, Reddit, Snapchat and massively multiplayer online games serve to augment the bars, cafés and other physical public gathering spaces previous generations had to visit to stay connected to their communities. The internet permits remote technical interactivity while also facilitating social interaction, Tai observed. Humans can use the "fourth place" to maintain relationships in our first, second and third places.

For journalists, the web makes it possible to carry all products of news on one platform—print and broadcast reports, as well as the public conversations prompted by the news. Discussions in the virtual town squares of cyberspace are uniquely enhanced by the internet's information storage and retrieval capabilities, which give participants access to material otherwise unavailable, observed Zizi Papacharissi. The web's ability to disseminate news and facilitate collaboration and updates is faster and more far reaching than any other medium. Whether the public gathering places of the digital space transcend adequately into "public spheres" however, is not the responsibility of the technology, Papacharissi argues. The responsibility rests with the people who communicate in cyberspace.[24] That includes news purveyors and members of the audience.

Mainstream news organizations have traditionally occupied two important roles in contributing to a dynamic public sphere. Their first duty—the reporting of news—ensures the citizenry has access to reliable information to make informed arguments and decisions. Professional journalists are trained to solicit a diverse set of perspectives from those affected by a news story during the newsgathering process. Because it is impossible for any single journalist or news organization to represent every possible position on an issue, and because journalists independently decide which information to amplify or exclude, the potential for bias can creep into the newsgathering process. To counterbalance any partiality, news outlets can activate a second civic role: providing a forum for public discourse.[25] Through mediated public forums, news outlets open up opportunities for additional voices and views to be combined with journalist-generated information, leading to greater and more balanced insights for the public.

News organizations are not required to host online comments, but they have been expected throughout American history as part of their journalistic responsibility to provide a voice for the public in some form. In 1947, the U.S. Commission on Freedom of the Press, also known as the Hutchins Commission, declared that a "forum for the exchange of comment and criticism" is one of the requirements "society is entitled to demand of its press."[26]

What constitutes a public forum hosted by a news purveyor can vary. For example, space can be designated for letters to the editor or op-ed contributions from multiple sides of the political spectrum. News organizations can host or sponsor citizen gatherings such as live town hall events, talks or salons to incorporate and capture diverse audience input and then publicize the ideas discussed. News sites can also commit to ongoing coverage of actual citizen problem solving, including the results of public conversations on issues of concern and the immediate and long-term impact on participants. The modern public forum model with the lowest overhead for news organizations and the lowest barrier of entry for the audience is the computer-mediated collection of online comments and other types of digital user-generated content in the "fourth place."

In offering the public story-specific feedback channels attached to digital news content, news organizations pushed forward the "evolution of participatory spaces" and the "responsiveness of news."[27] Whereas the one-to-many structure of traditional print and broadcast media discouraged two-way communication with the audience and inhibited "marginal notation and group discussion," online media encourage all these actions.[28] Journalists can view comments posted in online venues of expression as virtual representations of public discourse, where individual citizens as democratic actors "decide when and how to voice their political convictions."[29] By soliciting, publishing and amplifying public "talk backs," news purveyors arguably make online comments into another "product" of journalism.

When audience members pose unanswered questions or present well-informed counterpoints in feedback forums, the resulting collaboration adds value to citizens' and journalists' understanding of the news topic. Authentic comments provide journalists and readers and viewers with a deeper sense of how a story, a photo, a video, a data visualization or other work of journalism resonates. Digital conversations hosted by news purveyors may also be utilized to connect communities fragmented by geographic distance and, in the best scenario, break down ideological barriers between groups and individuals. Comment sections on news sites, when welcoming, form new communities. Community organizing is democracy in action.[30]

One of my favorite examples of virtual community formation is the crossword puzzle enthusiasts who developed sustained relationships through interaction in the comments section of *The Guardian* daily digital crossword puzzles. "They've gotten to know the day to day of each other's lives—all through their love for word puzzles," reported *The Observer's* Sage Lazzaro. "The puzzles have transformed into a virtual hangout of sorts, complete with like-minded individuals, friendly conversation and some entertainment on the side."[31]

The democratic writings of Alexis de Tocqueville and John Stuart Mill suggest that when citizens discuss public problems together, they come to place more value upon the interests of the broader community and build a sense of "public spiritedness," explains political scientist James Fishkin.[32] Community discussions on the World Wide Web also make up an important component of "the digital commons." In her book *Consent of the Networked*, Rebecca MacKinnon refers to the digital commons as the virtual equivalent of de Tocqueville's vibrant civil society through which citizens share ideas, form associations to solve problems and push back against perceived infringements of their rights.[33]

News Conversations and Deliberative Democracy

Professional news reports and the public's discourse work together to facilitate what political theorists call deliberative democracy. To borrow a definition from political scientists Joohan Kim, Robert O. Wyatt and Elihu Katz, deliberative democracy refers to a political system that centers on citizens' free discussion of public issues. It can be powered by the interrelationships of news media use, political conversation, opinion formation and political participation.[34] Deliberative democracy asserts political decisions should be the product of fair and rational debate among citizens. "Deliberation" is defined here as a free exchange of arguments and practical reasoning that has the ability to change preferences and opinions.[35]

Deliberative democracy as a political system is considered "discursive" because citizen activities of sharing information, conversing, forming opinions and participating all incorporate characteristics of discourse and communicative action.[36] The system embraces the formal discourse practices of legislative bodies and institutions, as well as the "culture of free discussion and voluntary participation" among ordinary citizens.[37]

Much like the software developers on Agile teams, deliberative democracy puts a stronger emphasis on the iterative awakenings of the decision-making process than on the ultimate outcome. In a deliberative democracy, citizens are supposed to arrive at political decisions through reason and the collection of competing viewpoints—by engaging in focused conversations, considering various claims designed to secure the public good and reaching consensus. Political theorists argue the back-and-forth of civil discussion is necessary for the legitimacy of democratic political decisions.

If conversation is the underpinning of deliberation, then news has historically served as a universal trigger of conversation. News provides the public with the conversational topics of the day.[38] French sociologist Gabriel Tarde noted as far back as the 1890s that newspaper articles had the capacity to stimulate conversations among people at the interpersonal level.[39] "Informal conversations among acquaintances" about happenings reported in the news can shape democracy as much as formal deliberation and debate in legislative assemblies or civic organizations.[40] It is within casual discussions, informal deliberation and spirited interpersonal arguments that political theorists say "democratic culture receives its most concrete realization."[41]

Tarde noted the informal news-related public debates happening in cafés and salons served as a crucial intermediary between press coverage of the agendas of politicians and other elites and a reasoned public opinion.[42] As political scientist Susan Herbst puts it, Tarde recognized the multiple roles the press plays in both initiating conversations among citizens and serving as a "weathervane" sensing the shifting directions of public opinion.[43] Herbst also points to the ideas of Ferdinand Tonnies, an early-20th-century German sociologist, who determined three forms of "public opinion" observable in the citizenry: discussions or debates, public behavior such as rallies or protests and the content of newspapers.

"People get information about policy from media," explained Herbst, "and media professionals are 'sensors' who can gauge public reaction, and report this information on public reaction back to readers/viewers, lawmakers, interest group leaders and the like."[44] Herbst argues that public opinion possesses a dual nature: opinion formation and the expression it generates. The media drive the expression part—the conversation—and shape and report on it.

Research by Kim, Wyatt, and Katz suggests news media use is closely associated with the frequency of political conversation in daily life at both general and issue-specific levels. The willingness to argue with those who have different opinions is influenced by news media use and political talk. News media use and political conversation are also shown to have positive effects on the quality of arguments, opinions and opinion consistency. In addition, Kim, Wyatt and Katz determined news media use and political conversation are closely associated with participatory activities, such as "campaigning" and "complaining." Complaining is a frequent occurrence in online comment sections.[45]

The power of news to make an impact in a democracy begins when it starts conversations and elicits "user stories." Add the internet to the public discourse equation, and the primary function of professional journalism to provide a "public forum for dialogue among citizens and serve as a common carrier of the perspectives of varied groups in society" comes starkly into view.[46] As sociologist Michael Schudson explained, "The internet opens up this journalistic function in the most wide-ranging and profound way. Its virtue is not individual but social: the virtue of interaction, of conversation, of an easy and agreeable democratic sociability."

With networked conversations in the "fourth place" linked to news, the scale of social organization and knowledge exchange has expanded immensely.[47] Uniting specific news content with user comments enables political pluralism to be expressed by amplifying differing views and ideological approaches.[48] The internet affords more participation opportunities to more people, such as those who otherwise find too much discomfort in talking about politics in their own face-to-face environments[49] or within their own immediate net-worked social circles.[50] The anonymous nature of online commenting, which will be discussed in Chapter 4, helps in this regard.

Yet nothing constructive in this ideal democratic–digital news–conversation landscape comes easy for journalists. While automated online comment sections are the easiest type of public forum for news organizations to construct for discourse, the quality of public contributions collected from unmoderated forums is wretchedly problematic. They don't do much to build a culture of dialogue and deliberation or promote citizen engagement. When an open comment system is affixed to a hot-button, high-interest topic, the digital feedback area can generate a crushing volume of audience responses, many of which are stained with incivility and misinformation. Specific examples of how the most vexing obstacles of participatory journalism have escalated in the last decade will be explored in the next chapter.

Digital Journalism Is a Conversation

> When an audience do not complain, it is a compliment, and when they do it is a compliment, too, if unaccompanied by violence.
> —Mark Twain, *Letter to George W. Cable*, Jan. 15, 1883[51]

While "conversation" has roots in democratic theory, the concept of journalism-as-a-conversation also pertains to audience participation in news creation.[52] Digital discussion forums constitute a form of "collaboration" with news audiences—not just informing but involving readers and viewers.[53] Online comments and social media exchanges allow "the people formerly known as the audience" to be not just passive consumers of news and information but generators of it as well.[54]

The modern read-write information ecosystem means that "news is no longer a product delivered by one cohort—journalists—consumed largely in private by another—audiences—who then interact with each other in a mostly . . . invisible way around a proverbial water cooler," explained Tom Rosenstiel. "The new journalism has the potential to be a more dynamic interaction between these cohorts and at its best even a virtuous circle of learning."[55]

Since the public gained access to the internet as a communication channel in 1995, media critics such as Dan Gillmor have stressed the digital iteration of news should be more of a conversation or a seminar rather than a lecture.[56] "A more expressive public presents a new set of challenges to journalism, but it also demands that we revisit journalism's core purpose," explained Monica Guzman. "Can our purpose be just to inform, when people are so adept at informing themselves? Can our purpose be just to report facts and context, when so much of what drives our society are the stories people tell each other, stories a whole army of journalists could never hope to find and report themselves?"[57]

Surveying the public's online commentary has become a necessity in the practice of real-time journalism. By widening the disclosure circle of information sharing, open internet communication channels contribute to journalists' truth-finding process. Reporting on the public's commentary the conversational interactions of audience members, and the exchanges between citizens and journalists, is now a routine journalistic enterprise. Contemporary journalists are expected to augment news content and shape their professionally constructed public spheres with interpersonal contributions from the crowd.[58]

"The shift to online news is increasing engagement, adding more perspectives, and introducing more witnesses and a wider spectrum of voices to the media industry," Rosenstiel explains.[59] Rosenstiel's view of "news as collaborative intelligence" does not displace journalists in favor of "citizen journalists" or digitally networked technology. Rather, he argues that journalists, the public and technology are interdependent—each exploiting the unique strengths of the others in a symbiotic relationship.[60] For some audience members, an active comments section can make or break a news site.

Online commenting is a facet of what digital news outlets refer to as community or audience engagement, an area that has grown in importance as the internet has collapsed the distance between readers/viewers and news producers, and splintered people's attention through "democratized" information access and choice. As more democratic actors choose to communicate publicly through the internet, the torrent of digital exchanges—and archived access to those ideas and opinions—become key components of the democratic landscape and the practice of journalism. Topical comment forums appended to the bottom of news stories enable spontaneous and timely public discourse from engaged audiences on the issues of the day—topics that professional journalists deemed of highest importance.[61]

It is important to note how feedback forums affixed to news stories and social media posts grant audience members access to two significant lines of communication. First, readers can discuss their views with audience members interested in the same news topics. Second, they can also "talk back" directly to the journalists and the news organizations reporting the news items of concern.[62] Commenters presume their publicly posted contributions will be "heard" by the journalist/news organization. This increases their stake in the engagement. "Conversation can really add to journalistic endeavors and a sense of community," observed audience engagement editor Amanda Zamora, as "it gives [the audience] a reason to come back."[63]

Two communication processes also become uniquely integrated when people comment in public forums hosted by mainstream news outlets: interpersonal communication and mass communication.[64] While some commenters may feel as if they are responding to just one person or talking with a small group, in actuality, the commenter is publishing in a mass media venue, broadcasting to an extended news audience of "lurkers" who read comments without jumping in themselves.[65] This also ups the ante for participants of public online conversations, whether they are conscious of the higher stakes or not. Mainstream news outlets still command giant audiences in the fragmented virtual world.

In changing the dynamics of audience attention, the internet has altered the dynamics of "conversation." Venues for online speech have multiplied exponentially. "The public forum has grown bigger and more powerful than many journalists could have imagined," observed Guzman. "It exists in countless spaces well beyond the boundaries of journalism, on platforms where journalists share a presence, but do not set the rules."[66]

Changing technology proves it is impossible to limit public dialogue to stories or forums that can be filtered through the judgment of news editors.[67] There are myriad examples of ordinary citizens, businesses, public figures and public officials who are "breaking news" on social media channels such as Twitter and bypassing news outlets completely.[68] Significant early examples of news stories first reported on Twitter by non-journalists include the January 2009 Hudson River crash of US Airways Flight 1549, the start of the Arab Spring in December 2010, the killing of Osama Bin Laden by U.S. Special Forces in May 2011, the sudden death of singer Whitney Houston in February 2012 and the 2014 deadly police shooting of Michael Brown in Ferguson, Missouri.

U.S. President Donald Trump notably dominated the news cycle during the 2016 presidential campaign by regularly creating news situations with his many early-morning Twitter tirades.[69] "Twitter functioned as this election cycle's beating heartbeat," noted *New York Times* reporter Farhad Manjoo.[70]

"Horizontal media," as described by media technology theorist W. Russell Neuman, allows users to amend, reformat, store, copy, forward and comment on the flow of ideas, complementing the functions of the news media.[71] While many arenas of public communication online continue to be dominated and influenced by the mainstream news media, a flood of alternative agenda-setting actors—citizen journalists, public officials, public figures, campaigners, propagandists, marketers, trolls—are producing and publishing information in the digital commons, too. Institutional journalism has had to cope with a serious challenge to its social function: "activity parallel to its own."[72]

MacKinnon argues the digital commons can exist in a positive and symbiotic relationship with both government and the private sector. But when governments or corporations abuse their power or are unresponsive, the digital commons acts like public-interest journalism, "as a counterweight and support network through which citizens can carve out the necessary spaces to speak and organize and thus defend their rights and interests."[73]

Journalists have no choice but to become adept at monitoring conversations in the digital public sphere, like reporters listening to the police scanner. Reporters eavesdrop on public conversations, follow the digital smoke and noise, gather and confirm facts and, if need be, debunk rumors.[74] The journalist has had to become an interpreter, sifting through swaths of information and opinion before deciding on what to report. The proliferation of social media use, in particular, has transformed newsrooms, speeding up newsgathering and enabling access to wider ranges of sources and material.[75]

"Journalists know it is their task (and perhaps even their civic responsibility) to listen and observe conversation and social action already in motion," Herbst argued.[76] In the course of newsgathering, journalists have customarily used interpersonal conversations and citizen conversations as informal data points to broadly ascertain public opinion. By listening to interpersonal dialogue, sometimes prompting it, sometimes coming across it unintentionally, "journalists believe they are getting a feel for opinion on an issue, and the frames people use to talk about that issue, and a general sense of what riles people up and why," explained Herbst, who studied how political reporters make mental notes about the opinions expressed by citizens, the intensity with which they articulate positions and their perceptions of issue debates.[77] Now that the internet enables interpersonal and citizen conversations to happen on a massive yet specific scale in countless online comment forums, news purveyors can monitor, collect, examine and measure digital comments as public opinion.

Some readers, such as BBC News user Pauline Fothergill, wonder why something as seemingly ephemeral as online comments is taken so seriously by so many. Fothergill commented: "It is a bit of fun, slightly narcissistic, and provides enjoyment rather than enlightenment for many. Lighten up, do!"[78]

Comments are consequential because digital discourse reshapes the setting, the flow and the persistence of public dialogue. Chains of discourse and discussion help news content reach larger audiences. The public's understanding and interpretation of major events "often has less to do with the facts, as news organizations report them, than with the conversations that follow them online," noted Amanda Zamora.[79]

The power shift in the relationship between media companies and their users also puts a spotlight on online conversations, however flawed. Ubiquitous connectivity and a 24-hour online news cycle deliver a never-ending avalanche of information, misinformation, reaction, shock, surprise, disgust, satire, confusion, reposts/retweets, commentary, debate and speculation into the digital public sphere. Internet cynics argue the sheer volume of information coming at the public, whether true or false or useful or pointless, threatens to drown the citizenry in noise and encourages short-term thinking instead of thoughtful, thorough deliberation.[80]

Publicly accessible user postings in the immediate context of mass media content provide an "independent voice to viewpoints previously disenfranchised by the corporate media."[81] These independent voices can affect how participating and lurking audiences perceive and use the news content, in both positive and negative ways. Reputable journalists and their respective news organizations are justifiably wary of trafficking in reckless commentary that causes confusion or damage. Online comments are an ongoing source of consternation for many journalists, as public discussion appended to news stories too often veers off into in-fighting between commenters, hate-filled attacks on journalists or the subjects of news stories, or off-topic posts. Comment sections are venues of opinion expression that can infiltrate the broader public discourse.

The digital power shift revives the classic debate about journalism's role in democratic discourse between American philosophers John Dewey and Walter Lippmann in the early part of the 20th century.[82] It is a clash between top-down "professionals" and the new media of bottom-up "amateurs."

Lippmann did not consider the general public smart enough to deconstruct modern society's deluge of information, especially when it came to political issues. Lippmann saw journalism's role as an intermediary necessary to filter and translate the complex ideas of the policy-making elites.[83] Citizens' only role was to read the news and vote. Meanwhile, Dewey believed in the public sphere—that some citizens are capable of reasoned deliberation and debate and able to express informed opinions.[84] Once issues were thoroughly vetted by the public, the best ideas would be identified and reported on by journalists. Dewey also argued for journalists to weigh the consequences of the policies being enacted by the elites on the public.[85]

The inclusiveness of Dewey's philosophy comes across as ethically superior but naïve. Universal access to unregulated mass communication technology is not a sufficient enough condition for the development of informed and empathetic public opinion.[86] Meanwhile, the exclusiveness of Lippmann's position would appear to maintain the quality of news and information, but it alienates the audience.

Agree with Dewey and online comments in the digital age become necessary for the discursive function of journalism. Agree with Lippmann and shut audience participation down. In my view, the sweet spot lies somewhere in the middle. Journalists in the digital age should, within their means, enable safe spaces for public debate—acting as conversation leaders,[87] information verifiers and amplifiers of varied perspectives. Journalism must evolve to serve a newly important function in the digital public sphere: "adding value" to the public comments harvested from cyberspace. Guided by journalistic and democratic values, news outlets should work to make sure their public forums are truthful, diverse and productive.[88]

"The central question for the future of the mass audience is one of balance," argued Neuman, "a balance between the forces of cohesive central authorities and shared values, as opposed to the diversity and pluralism of the changing mass population."[89]

Journalists aiming to responsibly add value to the public's online discourse face the challenge of determining what digital speech is "expressive" versus digital speech that is "influential." Political scientist Danielle Allen explains that expressive discourse circulates within communities with shared identities, alliances, solidarities and network connections and has limited impact in isolation within those communities. Conversely, influential discourse is speech that flows out and through decision-making structures and can affect action.[90]

Taken together, Allen explains, influential and expressive discourse can make visible types of political participation that were previously obscured. Allen makes a compelling argument that the "flow" of information in the digital age holds much greater potential than the cyber-places where the discourse originates.[91] So many conversation networks exist within the modern digital public sphere—from formal political institutions and mainstream news organizations to social media and semiprivate networks. Informal discourse must pass through "sluices" in order to enter spaces where it can be converted into rational deliberation and influential speech.[92] Allen cites the volume, velocity and "viscosity" of discourse streams as powerful characteristics affecting the rate of any social change. She defines viscosity as the capacity of certain speakers to communicate effectively within the context of the greater sociopolitical environment. Dialogue imbued with viscosity can flow from smaller, isolated public spheres to wider, bigger ones. There are, of course, degrees of friction affecting diverse communicative flows, such as when speech originates from marginalized communities or within authoritarian regimes that threaten punishment for free speech.[93]

Journalists, news outlets and social media sites undoubtedly contribute to the speed of the flow. Local or national news outlets that direct audience attention to particular acts of expressive discourse within the public sphere can cause the commentary to become influential. Social media networks such as Facebook and Twitter also have algorithms that draw attention to the public's expressive discourse via "hashtags" and "trending topics" and subsequently render the discourse influential.[94]

Dialogue in a mostly unfettered civic "place without space"[95] where anyone with an internet connection can participate through digital publishing also means the public posting of many different types of discourse— from rhetoric to humor to "dark speech." The digital universe has forced us all to confront proliferating forms of humor and dark speech, which Allen describes as "anonymity, incivility, adversarial speech, rumor mongering, alienation, dangerous exposure, censorship and corporate communicative power."

Allen's conclusions suggest that hosting a public conversation may not be nearly as important as putting a spotlight on the influential or potentially influential expressive commentary that already exists in the digital commons. Her idea gives some validation to those news organizations that have eliminated on-site comments and now rely on third-party social media networks for audience conversation. Problems set in, however, when low participation and participation inequality result from mainstream news sites failing to provide public forums or lead civil spaces for debate. Participation inequality is an issue that will be explored in the fourth chapter.

Journalists can try to balance their imperatives of audience conversation and inclusion through feedback forum design and comment moderation. Not all members of the audience will feel compelled or comfortable enough to participate, but news organizations can offer civility and veracity as premium features of public discussion areas. Media and political theorists have argued that conversations and discussions gain "democratic value" only if they proceed as organized, discursive and critical civic discourse, and appear as more than just informal conversation.[96] Comment sections that maintain journalistic standards are more likely to attract reasoned debate while minimizing the greater harms of false information and bullying.

In her book *Reclaiming Conversation*, psychologist and media scholar Sherry Turkle notes that citizens of a democracy depend on legislative bodies for "sustained conversations," built up over centuries. Society counts on the idea "that their existence means there will be other days, other chances [to talk], because, in a democracy, certain conversations are a responsibility." Is this not also true for places of journalism? News organizations, as community leaders and intermediaries, should not give up on comments or conversations with the audience. By offering their own venues for sustained public conversation, dialogue can mature through practice and modeling and develop a sense of proportion. "When we reclaim conversation and the places to have them, we are led to reconsider the importance of long-term thinking," Turkle argues, "the virtual provides us with more spaces for these conversations and these are enriching."[97]

The goal for news organizations is to create spaces where online public discussions can "teach how conversation unfolds, not in proclamations or bullet points, but in turn taking, negotiation and other rhythms of respect," explained Turkle.[98] News outlets that take the journalistic principles of veracity, civility and inclusion as seriously as their responsibility to contribute to a dynamic public sphere are more likely to remedy—and capitalize—on the splintered nature of digital conversations.

Notes

1. Hare, Kristen. "At The Cincinnati Enquirer, Social Media Uproar over Harambe's Death Has Been Part of the Story, Not the Story." *The Poynter Institute*. 2 Jun. 2016. Web. www.poynter.org/2016/at-the-cincinnati-enquirer-social-media-uproar-over-harambes-death-has-been-part-of-the-story-not-the-story/414326
2. Higgins, Tony. "Getting the Most from User Stories Using Collaboration." *Blueprint Blog*. 28 Jul. 2015. Web. www.blueprintsys.com/blog/getting-the-most-from-user-stories-supporting-collaboration
3. Nazzaro, William, and Charles Suscheck. "New to User Stories?" *ScrumAlliance*. 19 Apr. 2010. Web. www.scrumalliance.org/community/articles/2010/april/new-to-user-stories
4. Ibid.
5. Cohen, Bernard C. *The Press and Foreign Policy*. Princeton, NJ: Princeton University Press, 1963. Print.
6. Benkler, Yochai. *The Wealth of Networks: How Social Production Transforms Markets and Freedom*. New Haven, CT: Yale University Press, 2006. 272. Print.

7. *Measuring the Information Society Report 2016*. Rep. International Telecommunications Union, Geneva, Switzerland. Nov. 2016, p. 187. Web. www.itu. int/en/ITU-D/Statistics/Pages/publications/mis2016.aspx
8. Batsell, Jake. *Engaged Journalism: Connecting with Digitally Empowered News Audiences*. New York: Columbia University Press, 2015. Print.
9. Kim, Joohan, Robert O. Wyatt, and Elihu Katz. "News, Talk, Opinion, Participation: The Part Played by Conversation in Deliberative Democracy." *Political Communication* 16.4 (1999): 361–85. Web. www.academia.edu/3261247/ News_Talk_Opinion_Participation_The_Part_Played_by_Conversation_in_ Deliberative_Democracy
10. Ibid.
11. Dahlgren, Peter. "The Internet, Public Spheres, and Political Communication: Dispersion and Deliberation." *Political Communication*. 2005. Volume 22, Issue 2. 147–62. Web. http://dx.doi.org/10.1080/10584600590933160
12. Chen, Gina Masullo. "Journalists, Get Thee to the Comments." *Nieman Lab*. Dec. 2015. Web. www.niemanlab.org/2015/12/journalists-get-thee-to-the-comments
13. Kovach, Bill, and Tom Rosenstiel. *The Elements of Journalism: What Newspeople Should Know and the Public Should Expect*. New York: Three Rivers, 2014. Print.
14. Kovach, Bill, and Tom Rosenstiel. "Journalists Must Make the Significant Interesting and Relevant." *Nieman Reports*. 15 Jun. 2001. Web. http://niemanreports. org/articles/journalists-must-make-the-significant-interesting-and-relevant
15. Tenore, Mallary. "Best Practices for Doing Community-Driven Storytelling." *American Press Institute*. 17 Mar. 2017. Web. www.americanpressinstitute.org/ publications/reports/best-practices-community-driven-storytelling/
16. Dahlgren, Peter. *Television and the Public Sphere: Citizenship, Democracy & the Media*. London: SAGE Publications, 1995. 8–10. Print via Google Books.
17. Habermas, Jürgen. *The Structural Transformation of the Public Sphere: An Inquiry into a Category of Bourgeois Society*. 7th Edition. Cambridge, MA: MIT Press, 1989. Print.
18. Wessler, Hartmut. "Public Sphere." *Oxford Bibliographies Online Datasets*. 23 Feb. 2011. Web. http://dx.doi.org/10.1093/obo/9780199756841-0030
19. Dahlgren, Peter. "Public Sphere." *Encyclopedia of Political Communication*. Los Angeles: SAGE Publications, 2007. 682–5. Print via Google Books.
20. Tai, Zixue. "Emergence of Network Public Opinion in Chinese Cyberspace." *The Internet in China: Cyberspace and Civil Society*. New York: Routledge, 2006. 163–71. Print via Google Books.
21. "Ray Oldenburg." *Project for Public Spaces*. 1 Jan. 2009. Web. www.pps.org/ reference/roldenburg
22. Ibid.
23. Tai. "Emergence of Network Public Opinion in Chinese Cyberspace."
24. Papacharissi, Zizi. "The Virtual Sphere: The Internet as a Public Sphere." *New Media and Society*. 1 Feb. 2002. Volume 4, Issue 1. 9–27. Web. http://journals. sagepub.com/doi/abs/10.1177/14614440222226244
25. "Encouraging Free and Open Debate." *Kaieteur News Editorial*. 5 Feb. 2015. Web. www.kaieteurnewsonline.com/2015/02/06/encouraging-free-and-open-debate/
26. The Commission on Freedom of the Press. *A Free and Responsible Press*. Chicago: University of Chicago Press, 1947. Print via Archive.org. https://archive. org/details/freeandresponsib029216mbp
27. Reich, Zvi. "User Comments: The Transformation of Participatory Space." In Jane B. Singer, Alfred Hermida, David Domingo, Ari Heinonen, Steve

Paulussen, Thorsten Quandt, Zvi Reich, and Marina Vujnovic (Eds.), *Participatory Journalism: Guarding Open Gates at Online Newspapers*. Malden, MA: Wiley-Blackwell, 2011. Web. http://dx.doi.org/10.1002/9781444340747.ch6

28. Neuman, W. Russell. *The Future of the Mass Audience*. Cambridge, England; New York: Cambridge University Press, 1991. Introduction. Print via Google Books.
29. Nagar, Na'ama. "The Loud Public: The Case of User Comments in Online News Media." Order No. 3460834 State University of New York at Albany. Ann Arbor: ProQuest, 2011. Web. http://search.proquest.com/docview/879043165
30. Smock, Kristina. *Democracy in Action: Community Organizing and Urban Change*. New York: Columbia University Press, 2004. Print.
31. Lazzaro, Sage. "Adorable Community of Old Men Chat in the Guardian Crossword Comments Each Morning." *Observer*. 7 Aug. 2015. Web. http://observer.com/2015/08/adorable-community-of-old-men-chat-in-the-guardian-crossword-comments-each-morning/
    Also, Cresci, Elena. "Get down with the Guardian's Crossword Community, Wonderful across the Board." *The Guardian*. 10 Aug. 2015. Web. www.theguardian.com/crosswords/crossword-blog/2015/aug/10/get-down-with-the-guardians-crossword-community-wonderful-across-the-board
32. Fishkin, James S. *When the People Speak: Deliberative Democracy and Public Consultation*. Oxford; New York: Oxford University Press, 2009. Print.
33. MacKinnon, Rebecca. "Rise of the Digital Commons." *Consent of the Networked*. Reprint Edition. New York: Basic Books, 2013. 16–17. Print.
34. Kim, Wyatt, and Katz. "News, Talk, Opinion, Participation."
35. Barbaros, Maria Corina. "Matters of Deliberative Democracy: Is Conversation the Soul of Democracy?" *Meta: Research in Hermeneutics, Phenomenology and Practical Philosophy*. 2015. Volume 7, Issue 1. 143–65. Web. www.metajournal.org//articles_pdf/08-barbaros-meta-techno.pdf
36. Habermas, Jürgen. *The Theory of Communicative Action: Reason and Rationalization of Society*. Vol. 1. Boston: Beacon Press, 1984. Print.
37. Kim, Wyatt, and Katz. "News, Talk, Opinion, Participation."
38. Wyatt, Robert O., Elihu Katz, and Joohan Kim. "Bridging the Spheres: Political and Personal Conversation in Public and Private Spaces." *Journal of Communication*. Mar. 2000. Volume 50, Issue 1. Web. http://dx.doi.org/10.1111/j.1460-2466.2000.tb02834.x
39. Tarde, Gabriel. *L'opinion et la foule [Opinion and the Public]*. Paris: Presses Universitaires de France, 1901/1989. Web. http://classiques.uqac.ca/classiques/tarde_gabriel/opinion_et_la_foule/opinion_et_foule.html
40. Schudson, Michael. "Why Conversation Is Not the Soul of Democracy." *Critical Studies in Mass Communication* 14.4 (1997): 297–309. Print.
41. Tarde. *L'opinion et la foule*.
42. Ibid.
43. Herbst, Susan. "Journalistic Views of Public Opinion." *Reading Public Opinion: How Political Actors View the Democratic Process*. Chicago, IL: University of Chicago, 2010. 89–123. Print.
44. Ibid.
45. Kim, Wyatt, and Katz. "News, Talk, Opinion, Participation."
46. Schudson, Michael. "News and Democratic Society: Past, Present, and Future." *The Hedgehog Review*. Institute for Advanced Studies in Culture. Summer 2008. Web. www.iasc-culture.org/eNews/2009_10/Schudson_LO.pdf

47. Levine, Rick, Christopher Locke, Doc Searls, and David Weinberger. *The Cluetrain Manifesto*. 10th Anniversary Paperback Edition. New York: Basic Books, 2011. Print.
48. Rosenstiel, Tom. "News as Collaborative Intelligence: Correcting the Myths about News in the Digital Age." *The Brookings Institute*. 30 Jun. 2015. Web. www.brookings.edu/research/papers/2015/06/30-collaborative-intelligence-myths-digital-age-rosenstiel
49. Stromer-Galley, J. "New Voices in the Public Sphere: A Comparative Analysis of Interpersonal and Online Political Talk." *Javnost/The Public*. 2002. Volume 9, Issue 2. Web. http://javnost-thepublic.org/article/2002/2/2/
50. Hampton, Keith, Lee Rainie, Weixu Lu, Maria Dwyer, Inyoung Shin, and Kristen Purcell. "Main Analysis: Political Issues and the Spiral of Silence." *Pew Research Center*. Internet, Science & Tech. 26 Aug. 2014. Web. www.pewinternet.org/2014/08/26/main-analysis-political-issues-and-the-spiral-of-silence/
51. Twain, Mark. "Mark Twain Quotations: Audiences." *Twain Quotes*. Barbara Schmidt. 22 Mar. 2000. Web. www.twainquotes.com/Audiences.html
52. Marchionni, Doreen Marie. "Journalism-as-a-Conversation: A Concept Explication." *Communication Theory*. 2013. Volume 23, Issue 2. Web. http://onlinelibrary.wiley.com/doi/10.1111/comt.12007/abstract
53. Batsell. *Engaged Journalism*.
54. Rosen, Jay. "The People Formerly Known as the Audience." *PressThink*. 27 Jul. 2006. Web. http://archive.pressthink.org/2006/06/27/ppl_frmr.html
55. Rosenstiel. "News as Collaborative Intelligence."
56. Gillmor, Dan. "We the Media: The Rise of Citizen Journalists." *National Civic Review*. Fall 2004. Volume 93, Issue 3. Web. http://dx.doi.org/10.1002/ncr.62
57. Guzman, Monica. "Make the News a Conversation." *Nieman Reports*. 28 Mar. 2016. Web. http://niemanreports.org/articles/make-the-news-a-conversation
58. Reich. "User Comments."
59. Rosenstiel. "News as Collaborative Intelligence."
60. Ibid.
61. Nagar. "The Loud Public."
62. Ibid.
63. Reid, Alastair. "3 Ways to Think More Creatively about Comments." *Journalism. co.uk*. 7 May 2014. Web. www.journalism.co.uk/news/3-ways-to-think-more-creatively-about-comments/s2/a556675/
64. Ziegele, Mark, and Oliver Quiring. "Conceptualizing Online Discussion Value: A Multidimensional Framework for Analyzing User Comments on Mass-Media Websites." *Annals of the International Communication Association*. 2013. Volume 37, Issue 1. Web. www.tandfonline.com/doi/abs/10.1080/23808985.2013.11679148
65. Ibid.
66. Guzman. "Make the News a Conversation."
67. Fishkin, James S. *When the People Speak: Deliberative Democracy and Public Consultation*. Oxford; New York: Oxford University Press, 2009. 15. Print.
68. Rosenstiel, Tom, Jeff Sonderman, Maria Ivancin, and Nina Kjarval. "Twitter and Breaking News." *American Press Institute*. 1 Sept. 2015. Web. www.americanpressinstitute.org/publications/reports/survey-research/twitter-and-breaking-news
69. Lee, Jasmine C., and Kevin Quealy. "The 331 People, Places and Things Donald Trump Has Insulted on Twitter: A Complete List." *New York Times*. 11 May

2017. Web. www.nytimes.com/interactive/2016/01/28/upshot/donald-trump-twitter-insults.html

70. Manjoo, Farhad. "Breaking Up with Twitter." *The New York Times*. 12 Nov. 2016. Web. www.nytimes.com/2016/11/13/fashion/breaking-up-with-twitter-presidential-election-2016.html

71. Neuman. *The Future of the Mass Audience*.

72. Domingo, D., T. Quandt, A. Heinonen, S. Paulussen, J. Singer, and M. Vujnovic. "Participatory Journalism Practices in the Media and beyond: An International Comparative Study of Initiatives in Online Newspaper." *Journalism Practice*. 18 May 2016. Volume 2, Issue 3. Web. http://dx.doi.org/10.1080/1751278080 2281065

73. MacKinnon. "Rise of the Digital Commons."

74. Batsell. *Engaged Journalism*.

75. Jewell, John. "How Twitter Has Helped the Emergence of a New Journalism." *The Conversation*. 4 Nov. 2013. Web. https://theconversation.com/how-twitter-has-helped-the-emergence-of-a-new-journalism-19841

76. Herbst. "Journalistic Views of Public Opinion."

77. Ibid.

78. "BBC Trending: Your Top Comments about . . . Online Comments." *BBC News*. 22 Aug. 2015. Web. www.bbc.com/news/blogs-trending-34009807

79. Zamora, Amanda. "Comments Are Changing. Our Commitment to Audiences Shouldn't." *The Poynter Institute*. 31 Aug. 2016. Web. www.poynter.org/2016/comments-are-changing-our-commitment-to-audiences-shouldnt/428399/

80. Malik, Om. "The Distribution Democracy and the Future of Media." *Gigaom*. 10 May 2011. Web. https://gigaom.com/2011/05/10/the-distribution-democracy-and-the-future-of-media

81. Ziegele, M., T. Breiner, and O. Quiring. "What Creates Interactivity in Online News Discussions? An Exploratory Analysis of Discussion Factors in User Comments on News Items." *Journal of Communication*. Dec. 2014. Volume 64, Issue 6. Web. http://dx.doi.org/10.1111/jcom.12123

82. Crick, Nathan. "The Search for a Purveyor of News: The Dewey/Lippmann Debate in an Internet Age." *Critical Studies in Media Communication*. Nov. 2009. Volume 26, Issue 5. Web. http://dx.doi.org/10.1080/15295030903325321

83. Lippmann, Walter. *Public Opinion*. New York: Macmillan, 1922. Print.

84. Herbst. "Journalistic Views of Public Opinion."

85. Dewey, John. *The Public and Its Problems: An Essay in Political Inquiry*. New York: H. Holt, 1927. Print.

86. Crick. "The Search for a Purveyor of News."

87. Owens, Howard. "Six Roles, or Job Duties, of Modern Journalism." *Howardowens.com*. 26 Jan. 2008. Web. http://howardowens.com/six-roles-or-job-duties-modern-journalism

88. Guzman. "Make the News a Conversation."

89. Neuman. *The Future of the Mass Audience*.

90. Allen, Danielle S. "Reconceiving Public Spheres: The Flow Dynamics Model." *From Voice to Influence: Understanding Citizenship in a Digital Age*. Chicago: University of Chicago Press, 2015. 178–204. Print.

91. Ibid.

92. Ibid.

93. Ibid.

94. Ibid.

95. Searls, Doc. As quoted by Rainie, Lee, Janna Anderson, and Jonathan Albright. "The Future of Free Speech, Trolls, Anonymity and Fake News Online." *Pew Research Center*. 29 Mar. 2017. Web. www.pewinternet.org/2017/03/29/the-future-of-free-speech-trolls-anonymity-and-fake-news-online

96. Ziegele and Quiring. "Conceptualizing Online Discussion Value."

97. Turkle, Sherry. *Reclaiming Conversation: The Power of Talk in a Digital Age*. New York: Penguin, 2015. 330–3. Print.

98. Ibid.

3 Discourse Amid Discord

> The smoldering wreckage of public discourse has always been out there; the letters to the editor page has long been a mask of sanity over it, assembled from bits and pieces into a simulacrum of reasoned debate.
> —*Chicago Magazine* assistant digital editor Whet Moser[1]

Practitioners of journalism in the internet age have had to contend with an ascendant online force: digital incivility. Although cybercommunication has been widely available to the public since April 1995,[2] the tone of public discourse in many corners of the web has not matured. Unmoderated public comment spaces continue to resemble the middle school antagonists from *The Lord of the Flies*—feral, cruel and juvenile.[3]

Vitriolic online comments are so common they've become a pop culture joke. Comedian Jimmy Kimmel has had celebrity guests reading "Mean Tweets" about themselves as a recurring segment on his late-night ABC TV show since 2012.[4] *The Newsroom*, an HBO dramedy that aired from 2014–15, had its fictional national news anchor Will McAvoy on a "mission to civilize" his network's ill-mannered anonymous online commenters.[5] And in August 2015, the E! Network launched a short-lived Friday-night show called *The Comment Section*, which entertained viewers by presenting the snarkiest and most stupid comments on popular websites.[6]

An unimaginable volume of public speech has been unleashed by networked, computer-mediated communication. Anyone connected to the internet can share their ideas, opinions—and discontent—instantly to a potentially worldwide audience, regardless of quality or propriety. ALL-CAPS blanket statements and self-righteous sarcasm make regular appearances in comment sections on news items about everything from politics and crime to sports and religion. Castigatory speech populates websites intended for user reviews of businesses and services. Conversation threads on topical forums mutate into ad hominem attacks and flame wars when disagreements arise. And while popular social networking platforms like Facebook, Twitter, YouTube and Reddit may be runaway successes in connecting communities of people, those sites also serve as conduits for rumors, public shaming, hate speech and terrorism.

When news publishers first moved online in the late 1990s, they followed the popular lead of Internet Relay Chat, AOL Instant Messenger and bloggers by affixing interactive forums to the bottom of news stories. Comments on news content were initially viewed as an internet-powered variation of newspaper letters to the editor and a novel way of creating engagement through an immediate and ongoing dialogue among news producers, readers and viewers. The "talk backs" offered cues to journalists about the interests and cares of audience members and seemed to provide insight into local or topical public opinion.[7] Commenters could engage directly with reporters and with each other to discuss the most important issues of the day.[8]

However, editors at many news outlets—including at my former employer *The Hartford Courant*—made the naïve mistake of expecting audience members to initiate and police their own robust discussions, presuming the audience was newly and better informed by the connected news content. But journalists soon discovered that open discussions beneath news stories, and later on social media posts, rarely developed into useful, civil or on-topic public discourse when left unattended. Anonymous forums in particular devolved into Punch-and-Judy fests of extreme emotions, insults, inane observations, conspiracy theories and spam.

Political scientists who study deliberative democracy describe how difficult it is to effectively motivate busy citizens in a mass society to become informed.[9] Achieving the ideals of inclusion and thoughtfulness in public discourse is an even harder climb. An internet-powered citizenry with a buffet of personalized media and virtual places to vent further complicates the equation of meaningful democratic participation.

Greater access to information via the internet does not guarantee a higher level of knowledge or understanding among the citizenry either. Research shows unlimited information choice and the manipulative algorithms of attention powering the most popular online platforms tend to reinforce people's ignorance and biases and create echo chambers.[10] As technology futurist Roy Amara warned in his well-known computer age adage: "We tend to overestimate the effect of a technology in the short run, and underestimate the effect in the long run."[11]

When news organizations began hosting open online forums, they may have intended them for public deliberation, but there was no guaranteeing the audience would use comment sections for that purpose. Chicago-area radio personality Steve Dahl was one of many professional communicators who railed against the "useless" commentary on the web. "Everybody is now an expert on everything," Dahl wrote in a *Chicago Tribune* column, arguing that the ease of commenting online dilutes the value of opinions written by professionals, who had to work hard to earn their "stripes" as communicators. Thoughtful, well-written comments get lost among the "musings of morons," Dahl argued.[12]

The writings of Thomas Hobbes, a 17th-century English philosopher and political scientist, provide one explanation for the uncivil behavior taking place in open online forums. Hobbes questioned how human beings can coexist when religious or traditional justifications of authority are no longer effective or persuasive. Where authority is lacking, Hobbes wrote, "our fundamental right seems to be to save our skins, by whatever means we think fit." In this sense, open digital discourse is like a primitive society.[13] Because everyone on the internet is equal, and equal in their capacity to harass, shame and intimidate one another, there is no natural source of authority to order exchanges or stop the unbridled dog-eat-dog hostilities.

Hobbes's assumption that people are incapable of coexisting without authority implies that human online interactions on news sites would benefit from signage, structure and incentives to participate in a deliberative way. But the tenor of public dialogue in the digital space is also influenced by an "anything goes" cyber-libertarian vibe that encourages the use of networks as a means of promoting individual/decentralized initiatives and subverting dependence on centralized/traditional authorities, including the mainstream news media.[14] This collective has a strong resistance to censorship, viewing interference as an authoritarian silencing maneuver.

Freedom of expression—which is defined as the right to speak, write, publish or broadcast whatever one wants without constraint or intimidation—is prized on the internet. First recognized in the Swedish Press Law of 1776,[15] freedom of expression also appears in Article 19 of the Universal Declarations of Human Rights. The declaration, ratified by the United Nations General Assembly in 1948, states, "Everyone has the right to freedom of opinion and expression; this right includes freedom to hold opinions without interference and to seek, receive and impart information and ideas through any media and regardless of frontiers."[16]

"Freedom of expression is largely a *fait accompli*," observed Mitchell Pearlman, founder of the Connecticut Freedom of Information Commission.[17] It is a cornerstone of civil society, encompassing civic and political discourse and freedom of the press. Pearlman said it is also essential to the concept of a "marketplace of ideas," in which people can ascertain the truth and value of competing ideas from the uncensored expression of those ideas.

The unrestricted exchange of opinions and ideas, however "noxious," is something America's founders were also familiar with when they provided the groundwork for freedom of speech.[18] James Madison wrote in 1800:

Some degree of abuse is inseparable from the proper use of everything. And in no instance is this more true than in that of the press. It has accordingly been decided by practice of the States, that it is better to leave a few of its noxious branches to their luxuriant growth, than, by pruning them away, to injure the vigor of those yielding the proper fruits.[19]

The internet celebrates and protects its disruptive culture of expression. "That's the spirit of the original internet," observed Craig Newmark, founder of open online classifieds site Craigslist. "Build something simple and useful to people for making their own connections and then get out of the way."[20]

In his book *Audience Feedback in the News Media*, digital media researcher Bill Reader points out that much of the criticism directed at the incivility in open online forums stems from sociopolitical elites—academics, journalists, policy wonks, special-interest advocates, career politicians and business executives. "Those groups are, not surprisingly, the most frequent targets of anonymous attacks and vitriol via those forums. Evidence suggests that such elitism is not shared by the broader public, who read and participate," Reader explained. "Media professionals and scholars who are 'seeking a return to civility in online comments' seem to pine for a fantasyland dreamed up in an ivory tower, and they wax nostalgic for a 'civility' that never existed in reality."[21]

To expect sustained respectful discussion online or anywhere else is perhaps to ignore human nature. "Go to a true town meeting, especially one during which a local controversy is to be discussed, and despite the trappings of decorum, one will still see and hear statements that could be considered rude, crude, and offensive," Reader argued.[22]

The internet reflects people's propensity for conflict and hate as much as it displays their empathy and desire to be understood. "Technology isn't the problem here," states a report from Pew Research Center on the Future of the Internet IV. "It is people's inherent character traits. The internet and search engines just enable people to be more of what they already are."[23]

Reader asserts a true "virtual village square" should reflect society as it is, not as intellectual elites might desire it to be. He explained,

Some might argue that those who want to express coarse views or use impolite language can easily find other channels online, which is certainly true, but that argument is shallow and misses the larger point— if news media truly want their feedback forums to be virtual village squares, they should be far more accommodating of views and language that are found in the village squares and town halls of the real world, much of it angry and impolite.[24]

When news sites shut down comment sections due to incivility or ban rude audience members from discussions, the internet reverberates with angry cries of infringing on free speech by "intolerant, snobbish cultural elites"[25] and "close-minded" "thin-skinned liberals."[26] The web's free-speech-no-matter-what dogma has been a far more powerful standard bearer in news site comment areas than professional journalism's discipline of verification or intellectual fairness. In the debate over free expression, *The New Yorker*'s Jelani Cobb keenly observed, "The fault line here is between those who find intolerance objectionable and those who oppose intolerance of the intolerant."[27]

Computer-mediated communication networks have given a voice to those who, in the preinternet era, may have felt voiceless.[28] Open access on most of the internet breeds a sense of entitlement in news comment sections, too. Audiences have come to expect immediate, unlimited, on-the-same-page participation. Self-described cultural provocateur Milo Yiannopoulos, a notorious "free speech warrior" who was permanently banned from Twitter in 2016,[29] summed up the online anarchist ideology in an interview with comedian Bill Maher. "All I care about is free speech and free expression," Yiannopoulos proclaimed. "I want people to be able to be, say, and do anything.[30]"

Online comments are powered by the media's "game of attention"[31] and a digital culture of saying whatever one pleases making it a constant struggle to restrain public forums from morphing into *Beyond Thunderdome* arenas of invective and mob rule.

Toxic Disinhibition and Endless Arguments

Thunderdome. How do I get in there?

—Max (Mel Gibson)

That's easy. Pick a fight!

—Aunty Entity (Tina Turner)[32]

As much as the internet has transformed the dimensions of conversation, it has also transformed the dimensions of incivility in public discourse. While an individual's feelings or opinions may be scattered and temporary in the offline world, sentiments become permanent, searchable and "taggable" once publicly posted online.[33] Online rudeness has more outlets than ever. Mean messages can be copied and distributed instantly to huge numbers of people. Anyone can initiate or receive the information. Postings can be discovered in isolation and out of context. The impact of uncivil speech can be swift and far reaching, especially if passed along through mainstream news sites.[34] Digital communication exchanges may happen in real time, yet posts can also linger indefinitely or reappear indiscriminately. The cyberlife of critical comments can be unlimited.

Conflict is inevitable.

People with access to the World Wide Web don't need professional news articles to make public comments.[35] Rants are posted in any number of places online, including blogs, user-rating sites and social networks. When people armed with news reports and digital publishing tools seethe with outrage, they post comments—everywhere. A dramatic example of this modern development happened in July 2015 after *The Telegraph* identified Minnesota dentist Walter Palmer as the hunter who paid $50,000 to kill Africa's beloved Cecil the Lion.[36] Shortly after the news broke online, Palmer's name began trending worldwide on Twitter. Furious users tweeted death threats at Palmer, started an online petition calling for "justice" and besieged the Yelp and Facebook pages of Palmer's dental practice with hateful comments and photos of dead lions.[37]

People also published contact information for Palmer's dental practice, his home address and phone number on social media—a practice known as "doxxing." The name "dox" is derived from personal "*doc*uments," and its purpose is to scare (terrorize) the offending party by exposing private email addresses, relations or other personal information. Those who engage in doxxing defend it as "a stand against 'bad' behavior, or as a sort of public service."[38] But it is a digital form of harassment and intimidation.

Dealing with commenters who are angry or impolite is easy compared to subversive online troublemakers. Online misbehavior—which is not a fundamental human right covered by our definition of freedom of expression—gets carried out in comment forums in creative ways.[39] There are those who are egotistically motivated to post comments on local and national news content to increase their own exposure, to cast the world in a particular light, to push themselves into the spotlight or to intentionally cause a public disturbance.[40] Some are just in it for the *lulz*.[41] Authentic audience participation is undermined by automated comment generators (bots), spammers and acts of "astroturfing"[42] and "reverse astroturfing." Astroturfing is an orchestrated and unethical marketing strategy that aims to create an impression of widespread grassroots support for a policy, individual or product, where in reality, little such support exists.[43] An astroturfer will use multiple online identities to post a flood of remarks intended to "manufacture bottom-up support from the top down." This can mislead the public into believing that position is the commonly held view, but it is actually "a plastic version of the real thing."[44] Meanwhile, "reverse astroturfing" is the attempt to make a legitimate grassroots protest seem fake.

There are unscrupulous or vengeful individuals who use public forums to post threats and libelous statements, which can drag news organizations into criminal cases[45] and defamation lawsuits.[46] Acts of "internet vigilantism"—also known as hacktivism, where righteous individuals or groups engage in grassroots action to enact justice like a digital Batman—and "media fuckery"—described by sociologist Whitney Phillips as turning the media against itself by tricking journalists into reporting phony, sensational non-stories—are both perpetrated using public online comment arenas.[47]

Propagandists also exploit open comment forums to influence public opinion. Studies of the online information landscape after the 2016 U.S. presidential election revealed that commenting forums, including those on news sites, were targeted as pipelines for propaganda. In March 2017, retired Gen. Keith Alexander, who led the National Security Agency from 2005 to 2014, explained to a U.S. Senate committee how online trolls and socially engineered bots were being synchronized to spread messages and false stories to promote cultural tension.[48] Another study found 20% of all election-related tweets in 2016 were generated by computer algorithms—"bots" designed to propagandize digital conversations.[49]

"[Comment] trolls' last laugh may not be that they have begun to force large sites to circle the wagons, but rather that they are so perennially gifted at distracting us from substantive conversations," observed sociologist Sarah Sobieraj.[50]

As influencers who amplify information, journalists have also unwittingly contributed to viral instances of "context collapse"[51] and incited online mobs by drawing wide attention to casual online speech posted by citizens. User comments dangling from news stories and social media posts generally come across as shallow, obscure and ephemeral. Yet under the right circumstances, an online remark can gain sudden popularity and become notoriously enduring, to the shock of ordinary users. Citizens who add their voices to the digital public sphere don't always realize that any public online contribution is imbued with the possibility of virality. For example, the massive public shaming saga of public relations executive Justine Sacco—chronicled by author Jon Ronson in his 2015 book *So You've Been Publicly Shamed*—began because of a journalist.

It was *Gawker* editor Sam Biddle who learned of an ill-conceived, seemingly bigoted Twitter post by Sacco in December 2013 while she was on a long, internet-free flight to South Africa. Sacco's tweet read, "Going to Africa. Hope I don't get AIDS. Just kidding. I'm white!" Biddle wrote a snarky blog post and tweet about Sacco's tasteless comment, amplifying her remark out of context to Gawker's much larger audience.[52] Within hours, Sacco—who had a mere 170 followers on Twitter—was a trending topic worldwide via #HasJustineLandedYet.[53] She was attacked mercilessly for months by a mammoth online mob. The fallout cost Sacco her privacy, her job and her sense of safety. The dramatic episode signals how the internet's attention economy can be manipulated by the sharing of "sensationalism and scandal and sympathy and all the other things that drive eyeballs,"[54] a tactic employed by journalists and trolls alike.

While technology can make some tasks easier for human beings—such as participating in public discourse—the introduction of any new technology invariably inspires new approaches to those tasks, explains media scholar Henry Jenkins.[55] The rise of internet technologies has created new mass ways of communicating. These new moments of communication practiced every day accumulate and then are enabled by wider collective practices.[56] New approaches—such as the daily use of social media, expression through memes and gifs, and online misbehavior—"become widespread only if the culture also supports them, if they fill recurring needs at a particular historical juncture," Jenkins argued. "It matters what tools are available to a culture, but it matters more what that culture chooses to do with those tools."[57]

Behavioral psychology research provides insight into why modern humans seem so comfortable acting in such aggressive and thoughtless ways in the digital realm. Psychologist John Suler gave a name to the lack of restraint in cyberspace, calling it the "online disinhibition effect."[58] In face-to-face interaction, the brain reads a continual cascade of visual and vocal signals, emotional signs and social cues. Most people involved in face-to-face and, on a more limited basis, voice-to-voice communication can immediately make use of these sensory cues to guide exchanges. Behind the wall of technology, however, people act differently. Due to the ease and detached nature of computer-mediated communication, people use digital channels to pusillanimously convey the unpleasant messages they probably would not have the guts to say in person. Distant abstractions are easier to antagonize than "living, breathing interlocutors."[59]

Online communication—including discussions in news comment forums and on social media—is asynchronous. There is often a lag between sending or publishing a message and receiving feedback. Ornery commenters can post digital grenades of incivility and then exit the virtual discussion, committing the equivalent of an "emotional hit-and-run."[60] The smoldering venom left behind can be traumatizing to those on the unpleasant end of the communication. Commenters who post rude language, harsh criticisms, anger, hatred and threats succumb to what Suler described as a state of "toxic disinhibition." Not having to look someone in the eyes and deal with their immediate reaction can make humans bolder, crueler and more foolish. Suler argues that online disinhibition causes people to act out more frequently or intensely than in face-to-face, real-time dialogue.

Asynchronicity is another drawback to the notion of "digital-news-as-a-conversation." Digital discourse is like the digital news cycle—it never ends. "Internet argumentation has no natural stopping point, instead only ending when someone finally cries uncle. That unlimited space often gives rise to a kind of debate that works through attrition of attention and energy," observed Hazlitt contributor Navneet Alang. "Arguing online feels like an exercise in futility. Rules of debate don't work well within a medium without limits."[61]

Virtual text-based discussions allow people to exercise elements of what Suler calls "dissociative anonymity."[62] Because people can't see or hear each other when posting in news site comment sections or on Facebook or Twitter, they can hide some or all of their identity or alter their identities. The online invisibility lowers their risk of consequences. The combination gives people courage to do things they otherwise wouldn't—in good ways and in bad. Suler points out that an exaggerated sense of self can also arise from being alone and posting online—a state that is further enabled by the lack of any online authority to inhibit or scrutinize choices.[63]

Our society's always-on-screen life erodes the human capacity for empathy due to less direct face-to-face eye-contact, argues psychologist Sherry Turkle.[64] Text-only communication devoid of other social cues usually comes across as angry. It is also rife with ambiguity. Text-based online comment systems lack social presence and the media richness of face-to-face or voice-based communications. Conversation is diluted or disjointed, so it doesn't feel as personal or humanistic. It is easy to misconstrue communication because it lacks context. As a result, device-mediated conversations allow people to become not quite sociopathic but "socio-pathetic," a term coined by author Kristina Grish, meaning cowardly, thoughtless and disrespectful.[65]

"The poverty of social cues in computer-mediated communication inhibits interpersonal collaboration and trust, especially when interaction is anonymous and not nested in a wider social context," explained political scientist Robert D. Putnam. "Experiments that compare face-to-face and computer-mediated communication confirm that the richer the medium of communication, the more sociable, personal, trusting and friendly the encounter."[66]

Digital incivility also blooms in part because anonymity in the online environment allows people to separate their cyberactions from their in-person lifestyle and identity. "They feel less vulnerable about self-disclosing and acting out. Whatever they say or do can't be directly linked to the rest of their lives," Suler explained. "In a process of dissociation, they don't have to own their behavior by acknowledging it within the full context of an integrated online/offline identity."[67] Suler theorized how some people see their online life as a kind of game, with different rules and norms that don't apply to everyday life, separate and apart from the demands and responsibilities of the real world. Anonymity in digital discourse will be explored further in the fifth chapter.

"Sending a message from a keyboard over the air to an undetermined audience provides a sense of freedom that can lead one to make comments that should remain private thoughts," observed media researcher Alfred Hermida.[68] "By the same token, that sense of freedom can provide a sense of fulfillment."

Discourse on social media doesn't fare much better. Research about sustained use of social media platforms such as Facebook and Twitter suggest they decrease our self-control just as they deliver a momentary spike in our self-confidence. This means that when online, people are tempted to behave in ways they know will hurt others, but they seem to stop caring.[69] Another study found writing and reading online rants on social media was unhealthy and that the people who do it are generally angrier.[70] And while platforms like Facebook eschew anonymity and impose "real-name" policies, research indicates that real-name comments on social media are actually nastier than unsigned commentary.[71] "Social media favors the bitty over the meaty, the cutting over the considered. It prizes emotionalism over reason," argued author and technology writer Nicholas Carr.[72]

The speed at which uncivil behavior appears to overwhelm a digital comment area can be compared to the "broken windows theory" of disorder within neighborhoods. Developed by James Q. Wilson and George Kelling in 1982, the theory's name is derived from the observation that a building with a few broken windows left unrepaired attracts vandals who will smash more windows.[73] The theory posits that one small incident of incivility, when left unchallenged, creates a public impression that disorder is permitted, which encourages more problems to escalate.[74] The appearance of disorder instills fear in the minds of ordinary citizens, who come to believe an area is unsafe and retreat from it. "Gentler souls move out, and troublemakers move in."[75] If civil society withdraws from a community—be it physical or virtual—it weakens the social controls and community cohesion that keep bad actors in check. The withdrawal lays the groundwork for the problems of online participation inequality and mob rule.

The proposed solution to the broken windows theory is to maintain a basic level of "crime fighting" and repair and maintenance to establish a social norm and discourage additional bad activity.[76] Such a solution could be adopted by news organizations in "setting the tone" for online discussions. Research by Kasper Welbers and Wouter de Nooy tested levels of "adaptation" between users of an internet forum. Their study showed online commenters will modify their communication style to match the tone of previous posters within the same discussion thread, as well as previous posts in other threads within the same topic area.[77] It's like good or bad peer pressure. The "linguistic style matching" is a sign of "bonding," relationship building and engagement in the conversation, all of which are essential to deepen digital discussions in public forums populated by strangers.[78]

Results from an Engaging News Project study also suggest when a journalist engages with commenters in a discussion thread, the interaction can affect the deliberative tone of the conversation and reduce incivility. Researchers partnered with a local television news station and measured the civility of 70 political story posts within the TV station's Facebook community of 40,000 followers. When journalists personally responded to commenters, incivility decreased by 17%, and commenters were 15% more likely to use evidence in their comments, results showed. The study suggests journalist involvement as a worthwhile "psychological intervention" strategy for better discourse.[79]

"Pinning" a thoughtful, authentic comment to the top of a comment stream may also help focus discussions and establish a more civil tone with a less labor-intensive newsroom commitment.[80] An experiment by J. Nathan Matias that stuck "rules" to the top of a Reddit discussion board resulted in first-time commenters following those rules 7% more often on average (from 75% to 82%).[81] Not a huge jump, but every bit of additional civility and focus in an online discussion can keep it from careening into babel.

Where Emotions Prevail

> We're all at least a little bit troll.
>
> —Laura Miller[82]

The conditions that drive information sharing online indicate emotions rule. Stories that make us laugh or angry or sad are more likely to be talked about and passed along.[83] Research shows emotional arousal in the audience facilitates information diffusion. The work of journalists has always been laced with emotional elements, such as news coverage of crime, natural disasters, human difficulties and triumphs. Readers and viewers empathize with people affected by current events or become heated when they disagree with the ideas, opinions or perspectives presented.[84] "Emotional involvement" is considered a baseline indicator on whether a news story connects with the audience "because the strength of most journalism lies in its potential not only to inform but to drive people to action."[85]

Digital editor Kyle Geissler of WISC-TV/Channel3000.com in Wisconsin said his news organization's worst experiences with online comments usually start when a "user gets so upset they start making personal contacts with us." When that happens, Geissler explained, "the user is emotional. Rational explanations are ineffective." The conversation becomes less about the news and more about personalities, "which is never productive," he said.[86]

Channel3000.com is a digital news property that attracts 20 million page views a month. News stories about "someone who clearly made a stupid mistake seem to get the most comments," Geissler said. "This could be a bad parent or a criminal. These offer the most obvious opportunity for judgment, which our users are more than happy to provide."

Researchers have been able to show that the human brain naturally supports empathy, but they've also discovered it *really* pays attention to conflict.[87] Negativity in news stories generally increases people's anger and anxiety.[88] This can transfer to the emotionally extreme expressions of opinion in comment sections. The most common reason why people comment is to express an emotion or opinion, according to results from a January 2017 survey of 12,000 online commenters by the Engaging News Project.[89] Comments certainly qualify as emotional, and people aren't always civil when acting on their emotions.

Do uncivil comments get audiences more emotionally involved with a news story or a news site? If any reaction is better than no reaction at all, then yes—incivility can spark engagement in an online story and its comment stream. But incivility does not appear to sustain engagement. More than a third of news commenters (34%) and 41% of news comment readers in a March 2016 Engaging News Project survey named argumentative comments as the reason why they avoid commenting or reading comments.[90]

What compels people to read online news comments in the first place? Studies demonstrate people's motivation stems from a dual desire to obtain insight and be entertained. The "entertainment" motive is the stronger incentive. Research by Nina Springer, Ines Engelmann and Christian Pfaffinger suggests a substantial segment of news comment readers—also known as "lurkers"—are spending time in online discussion areas to be amused and not to thoughtfully reflect or debate an issue. However, another outcome of their study indicated that while inflammatory comments at the bottom of news stories increased the frequency with which comments were read, the low quality of the discourse reduced readers' satisfaction with the experience. Occasional news site visitors felt even more frustrated and disappointed with poor online discussions connected to news stories and considered such participation activities to be a waste of time.[91]

In another study of the motivations behind human acts of "media-stimulated interpersonal communication," researchers Marc Ziegele and Oliver Quiring observed that the same characteristics journalists use to determine whether a story is newsworthy—including timeliness, conflict, prominence, proximity, novelty and emotional resonance—are also considered by audience members when deciding whether to leave a comment. "News factors" influence both the selection and retention of news content by audience members.[92] News-diffusion theories also assert that the more news factors an item contains, the more it will be discussed online. Breaking news, in particular, nudges online news audiences into greater participation, where they are "commenting, posting and sharing at moments when events are moving fastest."[93]

Online news engagement typically starts with an enticing headline or social media promotion that compels us to click on a story. Unexpected, light-hearted or irritating headlines that deliver an emotional punch tend to get clicked. Research shows people also click on stories that give them something to talk about.[94] A provocative comment on a social media post might also prompt us to click. An affinity or aversion toward the sources quoted might provoke us to comment. Reading the first few comments in a comment section can spur us to read more comments and respond to remarks or repel us from participating further. The credibility or popularity of the originating news site also influences our decision to participate, especially if we are seeking opportunities to socialize with like-minded folks or argue with the opposition.

Like our conversations in the offline world, the tone of each online exchange is distinct. Ziegele and Quiring's research points out that within the same news site, one discussion about a particular political news story can be polite and well grounded, while the comment stream on another article on the same issue might be heated and emotional.[95]

Former U.S. president Barack Obama, in lamenting the current information landscape in America, remarked "the capacity to disseminate misinformation, wild conspiracy theories, to paint the opposition in wildly negative light without any rebuttal—that has accelerated in ways that much more sharply polarize the electorate and make it very difficult to have a common conversation."[96] Interestingly, Obama happened to be one of the "sources" that attracted the most incivility in online comments in a 2014 study of 300 articles and 6,400 comments posted on the *Arizona Daily Star* newspaper's website over three weeks.

The study by Kevin Coe, Kate Kenski and Stephen A. Rains demonstrated that certain "sources" are associated with higher levels of incivility. Almost one-third (32.7%) of comments in response to articles containing a quote from President Obama were deemed uncivil, in comparison to 21.4% to comments to articles that did not contain one.[97] Results suggest incivility in online discussions is contextual and that both the topic and the sources explain its occurrence. The researchers concluded that incivility—defined as "features of discussion that convey an unnecessarily disrespectful tone toward the discussion forum, its participants or its topics"—is indeed a common feature of public discussions. More than one in five comments posted on the *Arizona Daily Star*'s website contained a form of incivility.

The most prevalent bad behavior was name calling, which happened in 14% of the comments.[98]

Other interesting results from the study of *Arizona Daily Star* comments indicated lengthier digital discussions did not increase the rate at which incivility occurred. That finding contradicts the popular belief that incivility begets more incivility. Also, people who commented just once were much more likely to display incivility than frequent commenters. Regular participants played by the rules more than the conversation interlopers. "Hard news" topics, such as articles about the economy, politics, law and order, taxes and foreign affairs, attracted greater amounts of uncivil comments. The one outlier was sports, which attracted the highest overall percentage of digital trash talk (29.8%).

Most notably, the study showed that when commenters were directly engaging each other in discussion—a sign of listening and reflection and the foundation of deliberation—they were more civil. "If websites are interested in promoting more civil discourse," the researchers recommended, "it appears that facilitating greater back and forth among participants might be wise."[99]

Notes

1. Moser, Whet. "Making Internet Comments Sound Smart Isn't Easy or Cheap." *Chicago Magazine*. 16 Apr. 2014. Web. www.chicagomag.com/city-life/April-2014/Turning-Internet-Comments-into-Dialogue-Isnt-Easy-or-Cheap/
2. Leiner, Barry M., Vinton G. Cerf et al. "Brief History of the Internet." *Internet Society*. Oct. 2012. Web. www.internetsociety.org/sites/default/files/ISOC-History-of-the-Internet_2012Oct.pdf
3. Golding, William. *Lord of the Flies*. New York: The Berkley Publishing Group, 1954. Print.
4. Kimmel Live, Jimmy. "Mean Tweets Playlist." *YouTube Videos*. 22 Mar. 2012 through 28 Feb. 2017. Web. www.youtube.com/playlist?list=PLs4hTtftqnlAkiQNdWn6bbKUr-P1wuSm0
5. Sorkin, Aaron. "I'll Try to Fix You." *The Newsroom*. season 1, episode 4, aired 15 Jul. 2015. HBO.
6. Holub, Christian. "The Comment Section Host Michael Kosta Talks His Favorite Type of Internet Commenter." *Entertainment Weekly*. 6 Aug. 2015. Web. www.ew.com/article/2015/08/06/comment-section-michael-kosta-interview
7. Domingo, D., T. Quandt, A. Heinonen, S. Paulussen, J. Singer, and M. Vujnovic. "Participatory Journalism Practices in the Media and beyond: An International Comparative Study of Initiatives in Online Newspaper." *Journalism Practice*. Sept. 2008. Volume 2, Issue 3. Web. www.tandfonline.com/doi/abs/10.1080/17512780802281065
8. Nagar, Na'ama. "The Loud Public: The Case of User Comments in Online News Media." Order No. 3460834, State University of New York at Albany. Ann Arbor: ProQuest, 2011. Print.

9. Fishkin, James S. *When the People Speak: Deliberative Democracy and Public Consultation*. New York: Oxford University Press, 2009. 4. Print.

10. Mitchell, Amy, Jeffrey Gottfried, Jocelyn Kiley, and Katerina Eva Matsa. "Political Polarization & Media Habits." *Pew Research Center Journalism Project*. 20 Oct. 2014. Web. www.journalism.org/2014/10/21/political-polarization-media-habits/

    Also, Pariser, Eli. "Beware Online 'Filter Bubbles'." *TED.com*. Filmed Mar. 2011. Web. www.ted.com/talks/eli_pariser_beware_online_filter_bubbles

11. Pescovitz, David. "Roy Amara, Forecaster, RIP." *Boing Boing*. 3 Jan. 2008. Web. http://boingboing.net/2008/01/03/roy-amara-forecaster.html

12. Dahl, Steve. "Steve Dahl on Comments." *Chicago Tribune*. 11 Nov. 2009. Web. http://articles.chicagotribune.com/2009-11-11/entertainment/0911100420_1_town-hall-meeting-opinion-cnn

13. Williams, Garrath. "Thomas Hobbes: Moral and Political Philosophy." *Internet Encyclopedia of Philosophy*. Martin: University of Tennessee. Web. www.iep.utm.edu/hobmoral/

14. Dahlberg, Lincoln. "Cyber-Libertarianism 2.0: A Discourse Theory/Critical Political Economy Examination." *Cultural Politics*. 2010. Volume 6, Issue 3. Web. http://dx.doi.org/10.2752/175174310X12750685679753

15. Buchanan, Kelly. "250 Years of Press Freedom in Sweden." *In Custodia Legis: U.S. Library of Congress Law Blog*. 19 Dec. 2016. Web. https://blogs.loc.gov/law/2016/12/250-years-of-press-freedom-in-sweden/

16. Universal Declaration of Human Rights. 10 Dec. 1948. United Nations. Web. www.un.org/en/universal-declaration-human-rights/

17. Pearlman, Mitchell. Media and the Limits to Free Speech in the 21st Century. University of Connecticut, Storrs, CT. 6 Apr. 2015. Lecture.

18. Policinski, Gene. "Drawing the 'Online' Line on Free Speech." *First Amendment Center*. 10 Jan. 2010. Web. www.firstamendmentcenter.org/commentary.aspx?id=22473

19. Madison, James. Amendment I (Speech and Press). Report on the Virginia Resolutions. Jan. 1800. Writings 6. 385–401. Web. http://press-pubs.uchicago.edu/founders/documents/amendI_speechs24.html

20. Peters, Justin. "Craigslist Is Ugly, Janky, Old School . . . and Unbeatable." *Backchannel*. 14 Feb. 2017. Web. https://backchannel.com/craigslist-is-ugly-janky-old-school-and-unbeatable-85206829cb90

21. Reader, Bill. "Gatekeeping in an Age without Fences." *Audience Feedback in the News Media*. New York: Routledge, Taylor & Francis Group, 2015. 168–77. Print.

22. Reader. Ibid.

23. Rainie, Lee, and Janna Anderson. "Future of the Internet IV—Part 1: A Review of Responses to a Tension Pair about Whether Google Will Make People Stupid." *Pew Research Center*. Internet, Science & Tech. 18 Feb. 2010. Web. www.pewinternet.org/2010/02/19/part-1-a-review-of-responses-to-a-tension-pair-about-whether-google-will-make-people-stupid/

24. Reader. "Gatekeeping in an Age without Fences."

25. Bokhari, Allum. "The War on Comments Sections." *Breitbart*. 27 Oct. 2015. Web. www.breitbart.com/tech/2015/10/27/the-lefts-war-on-comment-sections/

26. Patrick, Fennell. "Letter: Thin-Skinned Decision on Online Comments." *The Berkshire Eagle*. 29 Sept. 2016. Web. www.berkshireeagle.com/stories/letter-thin-skinned-decision-on-online-comments,186182

27. Cobb, Jelani. "Race and the Free-Speech Diversion." *The New Yorker*. 10 Nov. 2015. Web. www.newyorker.com/news/news-desk/race-and-the-free-speech-diversion

28. Vargas, Jose Antonio. "Storming the News Gatekeepers." *The Washington Post*. 27 Nov. 2007. Web. www.washingtonpost.com/wp-dyn/content/article/2007/11/26/AR2007112602025.html

29. Isaac, Mike. "Twitter Bars Milo Yiannopoulos in Wake of Leslie Jones's Reports of Abuse." *The New York Times*. 20 Jul. 2016. Web. www.nytimes.com/2016/07/20/technology/twitter-bars-milo-yiannopoulos-in-crackdown-on-abusive-comments.html

30. "Milo Yiannopoulos Interview." *Real Time with Bill Maher*. 17 Feb. 2017. HBO. Web. www.youtube.com/watch?v=lImHh7fqrQo

31. Malik, Om. "The Distribution Democracy and the Future of Media." *Gigaom*. 10 May 2011. Web. https://gigaom.com/2011/05/10/the-distribution-democracy-and-the-future-of-media

32. "Mad Max beyond Thunderdome." Written by Terry Hayes and George Miller. Performed by Mel Gibson and Tina Turner. Kennedy Miller Productions/Warner Brothers, 1985. Transcript. Web. www.imdb.com/title/tt0089530/trivia?tab=qt&ref_=tt_trv_qu

33. Solove, Daniel J. *The Future of Reputation: Gossip, Rumor, and Privacy on the Internet*. New Haven, CT: Yale University Press, Oct. 2007. Web. http://ssrn.com/abstract=1019177

34. Meltzer, Kimberly. "Responsibility, Credibility and Academic Influence: Journalistic Concern about Uncivil Political Talk in Digital News Media." *International Journal of Press/Politics*. Jan. 2015. Volume 20, Issue 1. Web. http://dx.doi.org/10.1177/1940161214558748

35. Fishkin. *When the People Speak: Deliberative Democracy and Public Consultation*. 15.

36. Alexander, Harriet. "Cecil the Lion's Killer Revealed as American Dentist." *The Telegraph*. 28 Jul. 2015. Web. www.telegraph.co.uk/news/worldnews/africaandindianocean/zimbabwe/11767119/Cecil-the-lions-killer-revealed-as-American-dentist.htm

37. Broderick, Ryan, and Tamerra Griffin. "People Are Flooding This Dentist's Facebook after He Was Named as the Hunter Who Killed Cecil the Lion." *BuzzFeed*. 28 Jul. 2015. Web. www.buzzfeed.com/ryanhatesthis/this-is-whats-happening-to-the-dentist-who-allegedly-killed?utm_term=.rm7VAaxrn#.hwmLKkJYg

38. Condis, Megan. "Opinion: Cecil the Lion's Hunter Becomes the Hunted." *Al Jazeera America*. Al Jazeera, 1 Aug. 2015. Web. http://america.aljazeera.com/opinions/2015/8/cecil-the-lions-hunter-becomes-the-hunted.html

39. Sternberg, Janet. *Misbehavior in Cyber Places*. Lanham, MD: University Press of America, 2012. 87. Print.

40. Aoun, Steven. "iPod and YouTube and Everyone We Know." *Metro*. Spring 2007. Issue 152. 166–77. Print.
    Also, Buckels, Erin E., Paul D. Trapnell, and Delroy L. Paulhus. "Trolls Just Want to Have Fun." *Personality and Individual Differences*. Sept. 2014. Volume 67. Web. www.sciencedirect.com/science/article/pii/S0191886914000324
    Also, Jun, Paul. "Don't Feed the Haters: The Confessions of a Former Troll." *99U by Behance Inc.* Adobe, 21 Apr. 2014. Web. http://99u.com/articles/25151/dont-feed-the-haters-the-confessions-of-a-former-troll

41. "Lulz" is slang term derived from the text speak acronym LOL (laugh out loud). More than laughs, it connotes a form of nasty online tricksterism that aims to rile people up into states of outrage. See, Holloway, Kali. "Internet Trolls Explain Why They Do What They Do." *AlterNet*. 22 Sept. 2016. Web. www.alternet.org/media/internet-trolls-explain-why-they-do-what-they-do
   Also, Singal, Jesse. "How Internet Trolls Won the 2016 Election." *New York Magazine*. 16 Sept. 2016. Web. http://nymag.com/selectall/2016/09/how-internet-trolls-won-the-2016-presidential-election.html
42. Romm, Tony. "The FCC Is Being Flooded by Fake, Vicious Comments as It Begins Debating Net Neutrality." *Re/code*. 10 May 2017. Web. www.recode.net/2017/5/10/15612864/fcc-net-neutrality-bots-spam-comments-online-government-rules-ajit-pai
43. Bienkov, Adam. "Astroturfing: What Is It and Why Does It Matter?" *The Guardian*. 8 Feb. 2012. Web. www.theguardian.com/commentisfree/2012/feb/08/what-is-astroturfing
44. Lee, Caroline W. "The Roots of Astroturfing." *Contexts*. Feb. 2010. Volume 9, Issue 1. Web. http://journals.sagepub.com/doi/abs/10.1525/ctx.2010.9.1.73
45. Dwyer, Kelly. "ESPN Aids Authorities in Arresting a Man Accused of Making Threats against Children in a Post about LeBron James." *Yahoo! Sports*. 19 Sept. 2012. Web. https://sports.yahoo.com/blogs/nba-ball-dont-lie/espn-aides-authorities-arresting-man-accused-making-threats-152742600-nba.html
46. Loeb, Pat. "Philadelphia Judge Issues Ruling That Could Give Anonymous Online Commenters Second Thoughts." *CBS Philly*. 5 Mar. 2014. Web. http://philadelphia.cbslocal.com/2014/03/05/philadelphia-judge-issues-ruling-that-could-give-anonymous-online-commenters-second-thoughts
   Also, Franzen, Carl. "Idaho Defamation Suit Latest Test of Limits of Anonymous Online Speech." *Talking Points Memo*. 5 Jun. 2012. Web. http://talkingpoints memo.com/idealab/idaho-defamation-suit-latest-test-of-limits-of-anonymous-online-speech
47. Phillips, Whitney. *This Is Why We Can't Have Nice Things: Mapping the Relationship between Online Trolling and Mainstream Culture*. Cambridge, MA: MIT, 2016. Print.
48. Saletan, William. "How Russia Exploits American Racism and Xenophobia for Its Own Gain." *Slate Magazine*. 31 Mar. 2017. Web. www.slate.com/articles/news_and_politics/politica/2017/03/how_russia_capitalizes_on_american_racism_and_xenophobia.html
49. Ferrara, Emilio. "How Twitter Bots Affected the US Presidential Campaign." *The Conversation*. 8 Nov. 2016. Web. https://theconversation.com/how-twitter-bots-affected-the-us-presidential-campaign-68406
50. Sobieraj, Sarah. "Let's Not Feed the Trolls—But Let's Not Starve Online Comments, Either." *Cognoscenti*. WBUR.org, 24 Oct. 2013. Web. http://cognoscenti.legacy.wbur.org/2013/10/24/no-comment-sarah-sobieraj
51. Stewart, Bonnie. "Collapsed Publics: Orality, Literacy, and Vulnerability in Academic Twitter." *Journal of Applied Social Theory*. 12 May 2016. Web. http://socialtheoryapplied.com/journal/jast/article/view/33/9
52. Ronson, Jon. "How One Stupid Tweet Blew Up Justine Sacco's Life." *The New York Times*. 12 Feb. 2015. Web. www.nytimes.com/2015/02/15/magazine/how-one-stupid-tweet-ruined-justine-saccos-life.html?_r=0
   Also, Walsh, Michael. "Journalist Apologizes for #HasJustineLandedYet Twitter Uproar after PR Exec's AIDS Joke." *Yahoo! News*. 20 Dec. 2014. Web.

www.yahoo.com/news/journalist-apologizes-for-hasjustinelandedyet-twitter-uproar-after-pr-exec-s-aids-joke-164616178.html
53. Vingiano, Ali. "This Is How a Woman's Offensive Tweet Became the World's Top Story." *BuzzFeed.* 21 Dec. 2013. Web. www.buzzfeed.com/alisonvingiano/this-is-how-a-womans-offensive-tweet-became-the-worlds-top-s?utm_term=.xy6PqWyMZ#.io8aymQPp
54. Stewart, Bonnie. "Something Is Rotten in the State of . . . Twitter." Personal Blog. 2 Sept. 2014. Web. http://theory.cribchronicles.com/2014/09/02/something-is-rotten-in-the-state-of-twitter/
55. Jenkins, Henry. "Confronting the Challenges of Participatory Culture: Media Education for the 21st Century." *MacArthur Foundation.* 19 Oct. 2006. Web. www.macfound.org/press/publications/white-paper-confronting-the-challenges-of-participatory-culture-media-education-for-the-21st-century-by-henry-jenkins/
56. Jordan, Tim. *Internet, Society and Culture Communicative Practices before and after the Internet.* London: Bloomsbury, 2013. 21. Print via Google Books.
57. Jenkins. "Confronting the Challenges of Participatory Culture."
58. Suler, John. "The Online Disinhibition Effect." *CyberPsychology & Behavior* 7.3 (Jun. 2004): 321–6. Print.
59. Wolchover, Natalie. "Why Is Everyone on the Internet So Angry?" *Scientific American.* 25 Jul. 2012. Web. www.scientificamerican.com/article/why-is-everyone-on-the-internet-so-angry
60. Suler. "The Online Disinhibition Effect."
61. Alang, Navitt. "The Internet's Endless Argument and the New Shape of Debate." *Hazlitt Blog.* 8 Apr. 2014. Web. http://hazlitt.net/blog/internets-endless-argument-and-new-shape-debate
62. Suler. "The Online Disinhibition Effect."
63. Ibid.
64. Turkle, Sherry. *Reclaiming Conversation: The Power of Talk in a Digital Age.* New York: Penguin, an Imprint of Penguin Random House LLC, 2015. 171. Print.
65. Grish, Kristina. *The Joy of Text: Mating, Dating, and Techno-Relating.* New York: Gallery Books, 2006. Print.
66. Putnam, Robert D. *Bowling Alone: The Collapse and Revival of American Community.* New York: Simon & Schuster, 2000. 176. Print.
67. Suler. "The Online Disinhibition Effect."
68. Hermida, Alfred. *Tell Everyone: Why We Share & Why It Matters.* Toronto: Doubleday Canada, 2014. Print.
69. Wilcox, Keith, and Andrew T. Stephen. "Are Close Friends the Enemy? Online Social Networks, Self-Esteem, and Self-Control." *Journal of Consumer Research.* 22 Sept. 2012. Volume 40, Issue 1. Web. https://ssrn.com/abstract=2155864
70. Martin, Ryan C., Kelsey Ryan Coyier, Leah M. VanSistine, and Kelly L. Schroeder. "Anger on the Internet: The Perceived Value of Rant-Sites." *Cyberpsychology, Behavior, and Social Networking.* Mary Ann Liebert, Inc., 2013. Volume 16, Issue 2. Web. http://online.liebertpub.com/doi/pdf/10.1089/cyber.2012.0130
71. Rost, Katja, Lea Stahel, and Bruno S. Frey. "Digital Social Norm Enforcement: Online Firestorms in Social Media." *PLoS One.* Public Library of Science. 17 Jun. 2016. Web. http://journals.plos.org/plosone/article?id=10.1371%2Fjournal.pone.0155923

72. Carr, Nicholas. "How Social Media is Ruining Politics." *Politico*. 2 Sept. 2015. Web. www.politico.com/magazine/story/2015/09/2016-election-social-media-ruining-politics-213104

73. Castree, Noel, Rob Kitchin, and Alisdair Rogers. "Broken Windows Theory." *A Dictionary of Human Geography*. Oxford: Oxford University Press, 2013. Print.

74. Wilson, James Q., and George L. Kelling. "Broken Windows." *Atlantic Monthly*. Mar. 1982. Issue 249. 29–38. Web. www.theatlantic.com/magazine/archive/1982/03/broken-windows/304465/

75. Hinsliff, Gaby. "Play Nice! How the Internet Is Trying to Design out Toxic Behaviour." *The Guardian*. 22 Feb. 2016. Web. www.theguardian.com/us/commentisfree

76. Wilson and Kelling. "Broken Windows."

77. Welbers, Kasper, and de Nooy, Wouter. "Stylistic Accommodation on an Internet Forum as Bonding: Do Posters Adapt to the Style of Their Peers?" *American Behavioral Scientist*. 17 Mar. 2014. Volume 58, Issue 10. Web. http://journals.sagepub.com/doi/abs/10.1177/0002764214527086

78. Ibid.

79. Stroud, Natalie, Joshua Scacco, Ashley Muddiman, and Alexander Curry. "Changing Deliberative Norms on News Organizations' Facebook Sites." *Journal of Computer-Mediated Communication*. 2014. Web. http://onlinelibrary.wiley.com/doi/10.1111/jcc4.12104/abstract

80. Alba, Davey. "You Watching, Twitter? YouTube Just Cleaned Up Comments." *Wired*. 3 Nov. 2016. Web. www.wired.com/2016/11/watching-twitter-youtube-just-cleaned-comments/

81. Matias, J. Nathan. "Posting Rules in Online Discussions Prevents Problems & Increases Participation." CivilServant Project. *MIT Media Lab and MIT Center for Civic Media*. 8 Oct. 2016. Web. https://civilservant.io/moderation_experiment_r_science_rule_posting.html

82. Miller, Laura. "We're all Trolls Now, for Better and for Worse: How the Internet Lost Its Prankster Lulz and Found Its Outrage." *Salon.com*. 9 May 2015. Web. www.salon.com/2015/05/09/were_all_trolls_now_how_the_internet_lost_its_prankster_lulz_and_found_its_ideological_rage/

83. Jones, Kerry, Kelsey Libert, and Kristin Tynski. "The Emotional Combinations That Make Stories Go Viral." *Harvard Business Review*. 23 May 2016. Web. https://hbr.org/2016/05/research-the-link-between-feeling-in-control-and-viral-content

84. Graber, Doris A. "Say It with Pictures." *Annals of the American Academy of Political and Social Science*. 1996. Volume 546, Issue 1. Web. http://dx.doi.org/10.1177/0002716296546001008

85. Sillesen, Lene Bech, Chris Ip, and David Uberti. "Journalism and the Power of Emotions." *Columbia Journalism Review*. May–Jun. 2015. Web. www.cjr.org/analysis/journalism_and_the_power_of_emotions.php

86. Geissler, Kyle. Email interview. 31 May 2016.

87. Sillesen, Lene Bech. "How Screens Make Us Feel." *Columbia Journalism Review*. Jul.–Aug. 2015. Web. www.cjr.org/analysis/finding_empathy_online.php

88. Park, Chang Sup. "Applying 'Negativity Bias' to Twitter: Negative News on Twitter, Emotions, and Political Learning." *Journal of Information Technology & Politics*. 2 Oct. 2015. Web. http://dx.doi.org/10.1080/19331681.2015.1100225

89. Stroud, Natalie (Talia) Jomini, E. Van Duyn, Alexis Alizor, and Cameron Lang. "Comment Section Survey across 20 News Sites." *Engaging News Project*. Jan.

2017. Web. https://engagingnewsproject.org/research/comment-section-survey-across-20-news-sites

90. Stroud, Natalie Jomini, Emily Van Duyn, and Cynthia Peacock. "News Commenters and News Comment Readers." *Engaging News Project*. Mar. 2016. Web. https://engagingnewsproject.org/research/survey-of-commenters-and-comment-readers/

91. Springer Nina, Ines Engelmann, and Christian Pfaffinger, "User Comments: Motives and Inhibitors to Write and Read." *Information, Communication & Society*. 13 Jan. 2015. Volume 18, Issue 7. Web. www.tandfonline.com/doi/abs/10.1080/1369118X.2014.997268

92. Ziegele, Marc, and Oliver Quiring. "Conceptualizing Online Discussion Value: A Multidimensional Framework for Analyzing User Comments on Mass-Media Websites." *Annals of the International Communication Association*. 2013. Volume 37. Web. http://dx.doi.org/10.1080/23808985.2013.11679148

93. Rosenstiel, Tom, Jeff Sonderman, Kevin Loker, Maria Ivancin, and Nina Kjarval. "Twitter and News: How People Use Twitter to Get News." *American Press Institute*. 1 Sept. 2015. Web. www.americanpressinstitute.org/publications/reports/survey-research/how-people-use-twitter-news

94. Kormelink, Tim Groot, and Irene Costera Meijer. "What Clicks Actually Mean: Exploring Digital News User Practices." *Journalism: SAGE Journals*. 22 Jan. 2017. Web. http://journals.sagepub.com/doi/abs/10.1177/1464884916688290

95. Ziegele and Quiring. "Conceptualizing Online Discussion Value."

96. Remnick, David. "Obama Reckons with a Trump Presidency." *The New Yorker*. 28 Nov. 2016. Web. www.newyorker.com/magazine/2016/11/28/obama-reckons-with-a-trump-presidency

97. Coe, K., K. Kenski, and S. A. Rains. "Online and Uncivil? Patterns and Determinants of Incivility in Newspaper Website Comments." *Journal of Communication*. 16 Jun. 2014. Web. http://onlinelibrary.wiley.com/doi/10.1111/jcom.12104/abstract

98. Ibid.

99. Ibid.

4   What's Civility Got to Do with It?

> I know what I did. I helped divide. . . . And I think all of us are doing it. We're doing it on Facebook, we're doing it on Twitter. We tear each other apart and we don't see the human on the other side.
>
> —Glenn Beck[1]

Most professional journalists and journalism educators would profess to have a preference for civil discourse, as indicated by the ethics codes, news values and principles statements that guide the news industry.[2] For example, the Society of Professional Journalists code of ethics recommends that journalists "support the open and civil exchange of views, even views they find repugnant." The Radio Television Digital News Association trains its newsroom leaders to "be challenging as well as civil" and reminds editors that "reasonable people can disagree, adding light and not just heat to the room."[3] The Online News Association's ethics guidelines state, "Journalists at point-of-view news organizations can certainly engage in civil debate on topics of interest, which can encourage discussion and serve to inform viewers and readers."[4]

Civility is an intent, involving awareness that the tenor of interaction with other people is not designed to make them feel insecure, noted Donna Schenck-Hamlin of the Institute for Civic Discourse and Democracy at Kansas State University. Willingness to repeat or continue a conversation is a measure of a successful interaction. "[We] think too often of conversation as a one-off event, and politics as a zero-sum game. It's not," Schenck-Hamlin said. "Issues are never over . . . so willingness to improve our performance in continuing the conversation is probably the best thing that can happen."[5]

Most mainstream news outlets maintain a basic level of decorum in the institutional tone of their reports and in the outside voices they choose to amplify in interviews, columns, op-eds and letters to the editor.[6] ESPN's publicly posted social networking guidelines advise its roster of talent and reporters to "at all times, exercise discretion, thoughtfulness and respect for colleagues, business associates and fans."[7]

In comparison, "the internet is on constant boil," noted *New York Times* technology reporter Farhad Manjoo.[8] The candor and stinging language most people shy away from in face-to-face communication have become standard practice in the liberated digital space. During the 2016 U.S. presidential race, Florida Sen. Marco Rubio equated the acrid rhetoric of American politics with online comments. "Our politics have basically become like the comments section of blogs," Rubio remarked. "This is what happens when political candidates talk as if they're people on Twitter. The result is now bleeding over into the broader culture."[9]

When people first started conversing with strangers in cyberspace, discussions tended to be smaller, disparate, anonymous petri dishes of virtual community interaction. Each online group developed its own sophisticated norms to guide participants. Some forums organically established communities of empathy and trust.[10] Others, like 4chan, rewarded disruption, profanity, shock and chaos.[11] But when virtual discussion forums expanded onto mainstream news sites, incivility became a dominant disruptive force fueled by mass media attention and comment section neglect.

Local and national news outlets, and social media platforms soon after, helped create a hospitable environment for digital incivility by granting rude commenters, and sometimes nastier online trolls, mostly undeterred access to large audiences in unmoderated comment sections. The presence of digital trash talk beside professional news reports played a part in normalizing cyberantagonism. Unlike newspaper letters to the editor, most online comments were not pre-moderated by professional editors. Submissions did not need to be eloquent, thoughtful, truthful or even signed to appear with higher-standard, professional news content. Publishing freely on news websites gave disgruntled commenters—and trolls—a fig leaf of legitimacy.[12]

Online antagonism broadcast to the masses without interference on news sites and social media allowed a backchannel of antipathy to rise to an offline overcurrent. The sheer volume of acrimonious comments displayed publicly online has influenced social norms to include that kind of communication more. Nearly three quarters of internet users say they have witnessed online harassment, according to a 2014 study by the Pew Research Center.[13] About 92% of respondents agreed the online environment was more enabling of criticism, while only 68% said it facilitated social support.[14] The study participants also specifically identified news site comment sections as a source of hostile conversations, stating:

- "Comments sections of news stories are full of personal insults and name calling."

- "Comments sections of news articles often contain some very racist, homophobic, sexist language."
- "In the comment sections of news articles, there are frequently those who resort to name calling when someone states an opinion that differs from their own."
- "Offensive or insensitive or ignorant comments in response to published articles or columns relating to politics, economics and culture."
- "A hate-filled response to a written article. There was no dispute of the facts, just verbal abuse."

Digital discourse has grown harsher and coarser in part because the mainstream media enabled it, displayed it and modeled it. Plenty of journalists using Twitter have joined the chorus of snarky commenters. In surveys, Americans have blamed the media for helping to create high levels of incivility that undermine faith in journalism and deepen the nation's political dysfunction.[15] A 2014 survey by YouGov found that 30% of Americans admitted to engaging in "malicious online activity directed at someone they didn't know."[16]

The ability for anyone to broadcast abusive and offensive remarks—often anonymously, on an ongoing basis and essentially free of consequences—has had a pernicious influence on civic behavior and a corrosive effect on deliberative debate. Digital "straight talk" by the people formerly known as the audience[17]—including the 45th president of the United States[18]—cracked open America's pressure cooker of political correctness. "The circulation of abuse through social networks fuels the psychological phenomenon of "social proof,"[19] when people take their cue from the behavior of others," explained digital media researcher Alfred Hermida. "Seeing others make derogatory remarks publicly makes it seem more acceptable to be rude and offensive. Social media are a mirror to the rise of sexism and misogyny in popular culture."[20]

Conflict, harassment, and discrimination are social and cultural problems, not just online community problems. As public comment arenas have evolved and devolved through the years, they have allowed more people to access venues for extreme expression and online arenas that reward derision and anger. If norms favor conflict, people are more likely to follow. "People, wrapped up in their intellectual egos, use turns of phrase reserved for the most emotional situations because subtlety has virtually gone out the window," wrote *Wellesley News* contributor Jody Wei about digital discourse. "[Conversation] devolves to histrionics and bitter sarcasm so that neither party comes away from the exchange with a sense of enlightenment, just reaffirmation of their self-proclaimed intellectual superiority over the anonymous Other. Neither side walks away having learned anything new. What we're left with is anger, if anything at all."[21]

Civility in public discourse may be an expectation of citizens in a democracy, but harsh words and critical speech have always had their strategic uses.[22] Demands for civility can be exerted by those with authority to deny power to those with none.[23] People who feel marginalized or alienated use incivility to fight the power. By causing offense and indignation, outsiders can grab attention for their causes.[24]

It's not as if rudeness isn't baked into the history and business model of the American mass media. It seems sanctimonious for news purveyors to demand decorum from the audience when, on numerous occasions, the media have shelved democratic notions of civility in favor of the overriding goal of "attention." Consider the oeuvre of editorial cartoonists. The most attention-grabbing drawings tend to be the ones that provoke the most outrage—which in one horrible instance led to violence and deaths at the French satirical magazine *Charlie Hebdo*.[25]

The talk radio and TV news industries have a lucrative history of divisive programming, laden with displays of emotion and incivility. Audiences have been shocked and amused for decades by the incendiary rhetoric of Rush Limbaugh, the crescendo of confrontational questioning on *Hardball with Chris Matthews*, and the combative crosstalk of *The O'Reilly Factor*. TV executives recognized that the deliberative ideal for political discourse—civility—makes for dull television. In the 1980s, President Ronald Reagan once characterized the shout-fests of TV's *The McLaughlin Group* as "a political version of *Animal House*."[26]

Incivility is entertaining. The biting satire of late-night TV shows such as *Saturday Night Live*, *The Daily Show*, *The Colbert Report* and Bill Maher's *Real Time* also helped make snarky political comments and conversational zingers fashionable well before the 140-character arrival of Twitter.[27]

Even the strict language standards followed by stodgy news publications have loosened in the digital age, due in part to the competitive pressure of online upstarts, whose appeal to modern audiences is rooted in an informal conversational style and blunt delivery.[28]

Yet public perceptions of incivility in the comments sections of a news site can sully a news organization's reputation by association. When the Engaging News Project conducted its comment section survey of 20 news sites, researchers found that those who "trust" a news organization more perceive comments sections to be more civil than those who trust the organization less. Incivility isn't good for community building either. Fewer than half of respondents in the survey said they felt connected to any other commenters on any news site.[29] Persistent incivility in news site comment sections hurts journalists' credibility as community connectors and reliable brokers of the truth.

Polarization, Information Distortion and Participation Inequality

> Americans of all stripes are having too many one-way conversations where the goal is to filibuster and not to listen.
>
> —David Plazas[30]

Digital incivility serves as the gateway drug to other complicated problems plaguing public online discourse: polarization, information distortion and participation inequality.

In July 2016, I spent two mind-numbing weeks reading online comments stimulated by news coverage of the Republican and Democratic national political conventions. What I witnessed was unshackled digital vitriol volleyed back and forth from every side. The "live chat" comments on YouTube live streams of the #RNCinCLE and #DemsinPhilly conventions were the most virulent, polarized postings I encountered—a torrent of fear, loathing, hype, snark, mistrust and "motivated reasoning."[31] Motivated reasoning is defined as how people convince themselves or remain convinced of what they want to believe by avoiding, ignoring, devaluing, forgetting or arguing against any information that contradicts their beliefs.

In the weeks following the November 2016 U.S. presidential election, journalists also perceived an "exuberant escalation" of online offense giving from the left and right in comment "combat zones" at the bottom of news stories and on social media.[32]

Journalists' desire to maintain communication with readers has been historically and remains today one of the basic tenets of journalism. "Online reader comments represent a new opinion pipeline," explained news media researcher Arthur D. Santana, "but are imbued with a polarizing tone."[33]

Polarized digital discourse feeds society's partisan divisions. According to the Pew Research Center, partisan animosity in the United States is deeper and more extensive than at any point in the last two decades. "Ideological silos" have grown more common on both the left and right, with liberals and conservatives disagreeing not only about politics but about where they want to live, the kind of people they want to live around and whom they would welcome into their families.[34]

As the tone of public discourse has grown more caustic, ongoing exposure to displays of uncivil discourse is seen as a contributor to the mass polarization of the electorate. "Uncivil discourse increases polarization by helping partisans think less of their opponents than they already did," noted

Diana C. Mutz in her 2006 examination of the divisive forces of the mass media.[35] The current dominance of television and online news in the information consumption habits of modern Americans suggests that the masses are being increasingly exposed to uncivil discourse.[36]

News sites that are not attempting to pivot the incivility into constructive, deliberative discussions are adding to the polarization. A 2014 study of online debate by Hyunseo Hwang, Youngju Kim and Catherine U. Huh found that uncivil online conversations can lead to a broader crisis in which individuals believe attitudes among the mass public are "more deeply polarized along party lines than those who were exposed to civil discussion."[37]

News sites also have to deal with a digital communication phenomenon called "the nasty effect." A 2013 study by researchers at the University of Wisconsin–Madison and George Mason University found that rude comments on news articles often changed the way people interpreted the news story itself. The meaner the comments, the more polarized readers became about the contents of the article.[38] "People that were exposed to the polite comments didn't change their views really about the issue covering the story," explained Dominique Brossard, one of the study's coauthors. "The people that did see the rude comments became polarized. . . . It seems that rudeness and incivility is used as a mental shortcut to make sense of those complicated issues."[39]

Comments have the ability to color people's perception of the news.[40] A 2012 study showed that people who read an article without comments found it impartial, but when user comments that clashed with their own personal opinions were appended to the story, it raised suspicions of media bias, another communication phenomenon known as "the hostile media effect."[41] The commentary changed interpretation of the facts. When readers are impassioned about an issue, they are on high alert for media bias—real or perceived. If audience members' own views and those of online commenters are in discord, people can become defensive, assuming the news coverage swayed the others and, therefore, must be biased. Aligning news and comments forums together online can also cause some audience members to jumble the two and misremember authorship. Findings from the "hostile media effect" study suggest that news comprehension can decline in part due to user comments. There is also evidence that the likes, shares and comments of those we trust in our social networks not only facilitate the flow of "fake news" but help to affirm the validity of erroneous and misleading information.[42]

Because the social norm of polite discourse is not a widely practiced norm in the digital space, digital discourse is also suffering from a participation inequality problem. There are reasonable, informed citizens choosing not to add their voices to online discussions in the public sphere because of the hostility of comment forums, fear of public shaming by online mobs and the sadistic actions of internet trolls.[43] Often members of the communities being discussed in news stories and social media posts are not even involved in the comment sections. A 2016 study by the Data & Society Research Institute found that more than a quarter of all American internet users self-censor their online postings out of fear of online harassment.[44]

The miasma of abusive comments "have had a chilling effect on people's desire to contribute meaningfully to a productive discussion of the issues," wrote Kevin Moran, vice president of news for New England Newspapers, Inc., in an open letter to readers.[45]

Digital incivility that metastasizes into harassment and intimidation is a form of the "heckler's veto."[46] It scares away moderate, level-headed speakers from publicly expressing their views, while the most subversive, ideologically oriented and politically rancorous speakers siphon the public's attention. The toxic reputation of online comments has also impinged upon some journalists' ability to successfully land interviews for news stories. "Sources have objected to telling their stories for fear of reprisal in the comments," Moran wrote.[47]

While changes in interactive communication technology have enabled greater levels of participation, they have also strengthened hostile and prejudicial behaviors. Research by Arthur D. Santana suggests that anonymous comments on news sites bring out the vilest of views, especially on hot topics such as immigration. "Often the targets of the incivility are marginalized groups, including racial minorities," Santana observed.

When opinions move from civil and respectful discourse to vitriolic attacks on an individual, the fallout can be damaging—personally and institutionally.[48] The situation becomes nightmarish when nasty comments escalate into coordinated online and offline harassment within a community. This has happened at the local level, such as in Worcester, Massachusetts, in 2015 when residents who attended a community-moderated forum on race in the city expressed fear in continuing to talk publicly after one participant was targeted and harassed by online commenters.[49] It also happened on a worldwide scale in 2014 with #Gamergate, the viral internet culture war and "freewheeling catastrophe/social movement/misdirected lynch mob"[50] that shamed, harassed and threatened any critic who dared question the depiction of women in video games.[51]

The internet was supposed to even the playing field for participation, but women, ethnic and religious minorities and those who identify as LGBT experience a disproportionate amount of abuse in the comments. As a result, they participate in public discourse less often. When researcher Emma Pierson examined eight months of online comments on *New York Times* articles, she found only 28% of commenters of identifiable gender were female.

Pierson noted that women commented less frequently even though their remarks received a higher number of recommendations than comments posted by men. Her study also revealed that female commenters on *nytimes. com* were more likely to remain anonymous, and since anonymous commenters receive fewer recommendations, their worthwhile ideas were not as likely to gain attention.[52]

Media researcher Fiona Martin conducted a related study examining comments on the most popular online news services in the U.S., United Kingdom, Australia and Denmark. She discovered that at high engagement news sites, women made up at most just 35% of commenters and as few as 3% of commenters.[53] Martin's results matched the Engaging News Project's survey findings that show the majority of online news commenters are male and have lower levels of education and incomes compared to the "lurkers" who just read comments.[54]

The participation level of the overall news commenting landscape leaves much room for improvement. Half of Americans (50.7%) neither read comments on news websites nor have ever left a comment on a news website, according to the Engaging News Project survey.[55]

Jakob Nielsen's 2006 theory about user participation, known as the 90–9–1 rule, argues that in most online communities, 90% of the users are "lurkers" who never contribute. Nine percent of users contribute intermittently, while just 1% of users account for almost all the action.[56] Commenting communities, when left to their own devices, will not organically become representative of the overall audience. And constant feedback from the same 1% of users will distort public opinion from the 90% of users who are never heard from. Nielsen's theory asserts with only 1% regular participation, the "signal-to-noise ratio" also skews in the negative direction. "Discussion groups drown in flames and low-quality postings."[57]

Participation inequality will never disappear, Nielsen points out. "Your only real choice here is in how you shape the inequality curve's angle."[58]

According to a State of Community Management Survey, the average online community in 2016 was achieving engagement rates of 50% lurkers, 23% contributors and 27% creators.[59] But the 90–9–1 rule proved true for comments on *NPR.org*. When NPR eliminated its on-site forums in August 2016, ombudsman Elizabeth Jensen cited NPR's online audience metrics to explain the shut down. In July 2016, NPR's website recorded nearly 33 million unique users and 491,000 comments. But those comments were posted by just 19,400 commenters—less than 1% of the overall audience. Editors concluded NPR's commenting system was serving a miniscule slice of its overall audience and not worth the cost or headaches.[60] NPR audience members were encouraged to use social media for discussions instead.

But ceding conversations to social platforms doesn't solve any of the problems of polarization, information distortion or participation inequality. "It simply defers any solutions and puts the conversations about our journalism even further beyond our reach, shaped instead by algorithms that reinforce the very same polarization that bogged down the comment threads we couldn't redeem in the first place," argued audience engagement expert Amanda Zamora. "Social platforms are a key entry point—but that's where our engagement efforts begin, not where they end."[61]

Hateful Comments as an Occupational Hazard

> The comments section has become everything that other countries have come to believe about America. Every stereotype. Every joke. Every political cartoon. That we are mean-spirited, hateful, selfish crybabies who summarily shun anything that we don't understand. And I have to tell you. It's hard to disagree when you go to The Clarion-Ledger's Facebook page and read the gems that some leave under stories.
>
> —Brad Franklin, contributing columnist at
> *The Clarion-Ledger* in Jackson, Mississippi[62]

News producers often bear witness to or are directly targeted by the ugliest digital expressions of hate, harassment and intimidation from online agitators and the digital mobs they incite.[63] The cruelty displayed in digital discourse arenas is a cause of distress and vicarious trauma among journalists.

Hostile and virulent user-generated commentary has become an occupational hazard for journalists, especially for those who cover divisive topics. Reporters themselves have to worry about abusive comments from "keyboard assassins."[64] Contentious news reports or controversial opinion columns can trigger temporary yet potentially devastating surges of online aggression and outrage known as "online firestorms."[65]

"Comments are like working a second shift where you willingly subject yourself to attacks from people you've never met," noted *Guardian* columnist Jessica Valenti, who has been regularly abused online for her coverage of feminist issues.[66]

Female journalists and journalists of color have faced a steady, often brutal hazing from online commenters. They are targeted for abuse and attacked more than their white, male counterparts. In August 2014, the open, anonymous comment sections of feminist site *Jezebel* were flooded with animated GIFs of violent rape images. *Jezebel*'s writing staff protested publicly to corporate parent Gawker Media, pressuring the company to roll out an adjusted system in which comments must be approved before appearing.[67]

When the *Guardian* examined the 70 million user comments left on its site since 2006, results of their internal study revealed of the 10 most abused *Guardian* writers, eight were women and the two men were black. The *Guardian*'s analysis showed that from 2010 to 2016, articles written by women consistently attracted a higher proportion of blocked comments than articles written by men. Ethnic and religious minorities and LGBT individuals also appeared to experience a disproportionate amount of abuse in the comments.[68]

Helen Ubiñas, a columnist at the *Philadelphia Daily News*, expressed zero confidence in the existing system of online comments.

> I know I'm supposed to say that despite the trolls, I find some value in them, but I don't. I can probably count on one hand the times that I've found the comments useful or helpful or enlightening. When I do read them, which I try not to do, the comments quickly turn racial or political or both—even when the story isn't about race or politics. It also turns personal, targeting me as a Hispanic female columnist who is either a. a race-baiter, b. a race-baiting lib-tard or c. a race-baiting lib-tard who is obviously an affirmative-action hire. So, overall, I don't have much of a relationship with online comments or commenters.[69]

When the comments veer into venom on Ubiñas's columns, online editors will close or remove the online article's commenting feature. But determined individuals find other ways to communicate their enmity. Readers tweet at her, post comments on Facebook, call, and write to her directly via email and snail mail. Ubiñas said the most hateful trolls tend to call from blocked lines when they know no one is at the paper or email from anonymous accounts.

> I am still floored by the hate and vitriol and racism by commenters about people of color that I write about—even kids. It almost doesn't matter what the story is, it spirals into horrible comments generalizing a whole community or race or whatever. That, sadly, is viewed as par for the course with comments. And I think that's a real failure on [journalism's] part, in terms of moderating comments and civility.[70]

Ubiñas said her worst experience with comments happened when someone posted her home address online and suggested that people call cops and report a false home invasion—an internet vigilantism tactic known as "swatting."[71] She said,

> The point was to have the cops run into my house, guns blaring. . . . The un-moderated comment was up for like 10 hours. I probably felt most unsafe then, and exposed, and unsupported. It's a huge issue I have with online comments—journalists keep being told that there is value

in them, but I just don't see it, and I think it makes journalists very vulnerable at times. If news organizations value comments, then they should be moderated, vetted—for the sake of the conversation and for the safety of their employees.[72]

Ubiñas agreed that journalists should forge relationships with readers and that there may be more fruitful ways to create them in the digital space. "I see a glimmer of it, sometimes, on Twitter. Sometimes. But I think midsize news organizations continue to do an awful job with online comments and we keep being told it's a 'necessary evil,'" she said. "Journalists—not online editors or social media editors—have to take more control of their interactions with the public. For me, that means that I recognize that I am getting nothing out of online comments, so I try to build an audience, build a relationship elsewhere online."[73]

What constitutes offensive or uncivilized expression in the digital space can be a moving target. Personal attacks, harassment, hate speech and threats of violence clearly cross the line, as those kinds of nasty comments veer into criminality and render impossible the kind of substantive debate upon which any civil democracy depends. But there are subtler and sneakier expressions of incivility for journalists to reckon with, too, from hashtags to memes to avatars. Types of provocation found in comments include exaggeration, fatalism and simplification.[74]

In my views, what digital discourse needs is not elimination but a course correction. It's stuck in a spiral of negativity. Susan Herbst views incivility as a state of being rather than an ingrained personality trait. "Civility is emotional maturity, Herbst argues."[75]

Herbst's ideas are backed up by research from Stanford and Cornell universities that determined basically anyone can become a troll under the right circumstances. Researchers focused on how an individual's mood and the context affect what people write in online discussion forums. The changing moods people experience throughout the day can increase or decrease the likelihood of combative comments.[76]

"Just one person waking up cranky can create a spark and, because of discussion context and voting, these sparks can spiral out into cascades of bad behavior. Bad conversations lead to bad conversations. People who get down-voted come back more, comment more and comment even worse," explained senior study author Jure Leskovec. Findings suggest "that it's us who are causing these breakdowns in discussion," said co-author Michael Bernstein. "A lot of news sites have removed their comments systems because they think it's counter to actual debate and discussion. Understanding our own best and worst selves here is key to bringing those back."[77]

Journalists must accept that the troublesome incivility at the root of participation inequality, polarization and information distortion online is a permanent condition of public discourse. But abandoning public forums won't diminish the problem. Failing to protect or advocate for abused and harassed journalists, sources and audience members won't curtail it either. News leaders who acquiesce to online hate speech, misinformation and other forms of incivility end up sanctioning the bad behaviors. As Peter Dahlgren observed, "a system will never achieve a democratic character if the world of the everyday reflects anti-democratic normative dispositions."[78]

The digital hate that appears in the internet's mainstream and its prevalence will shape public expectations of online discourse, especially on social media networks populated with the young and impressionable, observed digital law scholars Danielle Keats Citron and Helen L. Norton. "Norms of subordination may overwhelm those of equality if hatred becomes an acceptable part of online discourse," they wrote.[79]

News organizations have enormous freedom in choosing whether and how to challenge digital hate and incivility. As private companies, news outlets are not only free from First Amendment legal concerns, they are statutorily protected by Section 230 of the Communications Decency Act of 1996 from any liability for publishing content or removing content created by their online users. By using nuanced approaches to hate speech, Citron and Norton argue, digital intermediaries can foster respectful online discourse without suppressing valuable expression. Well-developed and transparent online participation guidelines can address the meaningful distinctions between hate speech and other types of expression.[80] News outlets can then respond to the undesired speech in ways beyond just removing it. Journalists should challenge hateful speech by responding with robust counterspeech. News sites can also educate audience members about their own rights and responsibilities as digital citizens. Digital citizenship aims to protect users' ability to partake freely in the internet's diverse political, social, economic and cultural opportunities, which informs and facilitates their civic engagement. The news industry can do much more to empower and educate community members to champion norms of digital citizenship themselves.[81]

News purveyors are justified in reasserting their agenda-setting and gatekeeping roles to discourage incivility, Santana argues.[82] Perhaps the public's online "right to offend" can be balanced out with a revived journalistic duty to mend.[83] If online comments are "stirring the bitter brew,"[84] then journalism has an opportunity in the digital age to reboot its public-service mission by mindfully tweaking the existing recipe of online dialogue and providing the public with virtual places to talk with a key selling point: minimized incivility. In a "post-truth" reality, modern civil society needs more cyber-places for everyday digital discourse that's less about toxic venting and more about identifying common ground.[85] Professional news organizations should lead the way.

"Loud is not the same as logical," argued Rick Horowitz of the Association of Opinion Journalists. "Reasoned debate, informed debate, is a skill, a craft, a calling. The need for that remains as strong as ever—maybe even stronger, given all the competing noise in the room."[86]

Notes

1. "Strange Bedfellows." *Full Frontal with Samantha Bee*. Glenn Beck interviewed by Samantha Bee. TBS. 19 Dec 2016. Web. www.youtube.com/watch?v=wuSDfVRGI54

2. Society of Professional Journalists Ethics code: www.spj.org/ethicscode.asp; Associated Press News Values and Principles: www.ap.org/about/our-story/news-values

3. Radio Television Digital News Association code of ethics: www.rtdna.org/content/rtdna_code_of_ethics; RTNDA Leadership Book: www.rtdna.org/. . ./Updated_Revised_Leadership_Book_2nd.pdf

4. Online News Association Build Your Own Ethics Code: https://ethics.journalists.org/topics/social-networks/

5. Blomberg, Matthew. "Agreeing to Disagree: A Look at Civility in Political Discussion." Kansas State University. 23 Sept. 2016. Web. www.k-state.edu/icdd/CivilityVideo.html

6. Reader, Bill. "Free Press vs. Free Speech? The Rhetoric of 'Civility' in Regard to Anonymous Online Comments." *Journalism & Mass Communication Quarterly*. May 2012. Volume 89, Issue 3. Web. http://dx.doi.org/10.1177/1077699012447923

7. "Social Networking Guidelines for Editors and Reporters." *ESPN Front Row*. Aug. 2011. Web. www.espnfrontrow.com/wp-content/uploads/2011/. . ./social-networking-v2-2011.pdf

8. Manjoo, Farhad. "The Internet Is Breaking the Outrage Meter." *New York Times*. 10 Dec. 2015. Web. www.nytimes.com/2015/12/10/technology/shut-down-internet-donald-trump-hillary-clinton.html

9. O'Keefe, Ed. "Given Violence, Rubio Raises Doubts He Can Support Trump as GOP Nominee." *Washington Post*. 12 Mar. 2016. Web. www.washingtonpost.com/news/post-politics/wp/2016/03/12/given-violence-rubio-says-he-now-doubts-that-he-can-support-trump-as-the-gop-nominee/

10. Preece, Jennifer. "Etiquette, Empathy and Trust in Communities of Practice: Stepping-Stones to Social Capital." *Journal of Universal Computer Science*. 2004. Volume 10, Issue 4. Web. www.jucs.org/doi?doi=10.3217/jucs-010-03-0294

11. Dewey, Caitlin. "Absolutely Everything You Need to Know to Understand 4chan, the Internet's Own Bogeyman." *The Washington Post*. 25 Sept. 2014. Web. www.washingtonpost.com/news/the-intersect/wp/2014/09/25/absolutely-everything-you-need-to-know-to-understand-4chan-the-internets-own-bogeyman

12. Shanahan, Marie K. "How News Sites' Online Comments Helped Build Our Hateful Electorate." *The Conversation*. 14 Dec. 2016. Web. https://theconversation.com/how-news-sites-online-comments-helped-build-our-hateful-electorate-70170

13. Duggan, Maeve. "Part 5: Witnessing Harassment Online." *Pew Research Center.* 22 Oct. 2014. Web. www.pewinternet.org/2014/10/22/part-5-witnessing-harassment-online

14. Duggan, Maeve. "Online Harassment: Part 2: The Online Environment." *Pew Research Center.* 22 Oct. 2014. Web. www.pewinternet.org/2014/10/22/part-2-the-online-environment

15. National Institute for Civil Discourse. Web. http://nicd.arizona.edu/media

16. Gammon, Anne. "Over a Quarter of Americans Have Made Malicious Online Comments." *YouGov.* 20 Oct. 2014. Web. https://today.yougov.com/news/2014/10/20/over-quarter-americans-admit-malicious-online-comm/

17. Rosen, Jay. "The People Formerly Known as the Audience." *PressThink Blog.* 27 Jun. 2006. Web. http://archive.pressthink.org/2006/06/27/ppl_frmr.html

18. Lee, Jasmine C., and Kevin Quealy. "The 331 People, Places and Things Donald Trump Has Insulted on Twitter: A Complete List." *New York Times.* 11 May 2017. Web. www.nytimes.com/interactive/2016/01/28/upshot/donald-trump-twitter-insults.html

19. Cialdini, Robert B. "Social Proof: Truths Are Us." *Influence: The Psychology of Persuasion.* New York, NY: HarperCollins, 87–125. 31 Mar. 2017. Web. via Archive.org. https://archive.org/details/ThePsychologyOfPersuasion

20. Hermida, Alfred. *Tell Everyone: Why We Share & Why It Matters.* Toronto: Doubleday Canada, 2014. Print.

21. Wei, Jody. "Social Media Discourse Fails to Produce Substantive Results." *The Wellesley News.* 12 Apr. 2017. Web. http://thewellesleynews.com/2017/04/12/social-media-discourse-fails-to-produce-substantive-results/

22. Clayton, Cornell. "Anger and Division in American Politics." *The Blue Review.* Boise State University School of Public Service. 24 Oct. 2016. Web. https://thebluereview.org/anger-and-division-in-american-politics/

23. Skellet, Tim. "A Weapon for Liberation, and Oppression." *The Guardian.* 21 Jan. 2011. Web. www.theguardian.com/commentisfree/belief/2011/jan/21/civility-weapon-liberation-oppression

24. Shanahan, "How News Sites' Online Comments Helped Build Our Hateful Electorate."

25. "The Charlie Hebdo Attack: Three Days of Terror." *BBC News.* 14 Jan. 2015. Web. www.bbc.com/news/world-europe-30708237

26. Reagan, Ronald. "Remarks at a Reception for the McLaughlin Group." *Reagan Library Archives.* 29 Oct. 1985. Web. https://reaganlibrary.archives.gov/archives/speeches/1985/102985c.htm

27. Young, Dannagal G. "Lighten Up: How Satire Will Make American Politics Relevant Again." *Columbia Journalism Review.* 6 Jul. 2013. Web. http://archives.cjr.org/cover_story/lighten_up.php

28. Offitzer, James. "Watch Your Language: Swearing in News Stories." *American Journalism Review.* Philip Merrill College of Journalism at the University of Maryland. 4 Apr. 2014. Web. http://ajr.org/2014/04/04/swear-words-news-stories/

29. Stroud, Natalie (Talia) Jomini, E. Van Duyn, Alexis Alizor, and Cameron Lang. "Comment Section Survey across 20 News Sites." *Engaging News Project.* Jan. 2017. Web. https://engagingnewsproject.org/research/comment-section-survey-across-20-news-sites

30. Plazas, David. "Don't Let Civil Discourse Die." *The Tennessean.* 26 Nov. 2016. Web. www.tennessean.com/story/opinion/columnists/david-plazas/2016/11/26/david-plazas-civil-discourse/94277522

31. Kunda, Ziva, and Mark I. Appelbaum. "The Case for Motivated Reasoning." *Psychological Bulletin*. 1990. Volume 108, Issue 3. Web. http://dx.doi.org/10.1037/0033-2909.108.3.480

32. Bernstein, Joseph. "Alt-Right Internet Trolls Are Already Emboldened by Trump's Victory." *BuzzFeed*. 9 Nov. 2016. Web. www.buzzfeed.com/josephbernstein/alt-right-internet-trolls-are-already-emboldened-by-trumps-v?utm_term=.sfkmkl7rZ#.qyQG4kMmB
    Also, Bender, William. "Can We Make Comments Sections Great Again?" *Philly.com*. 10 Dec. 2016. Web. www.philly.com/philly/news/20161211_Can_we_make_comments_sections_great_again_.html

33. Santana, Arthur D. "Online Readers' Comments Represent New Opinion Pipeline." *Newspaper Research Journal*. 2011. Volume 32, Issue 3. Web. http://dx.doi.org/10.1177/073953291103200306

34. "Partisanship and Political Animosity in 2016." *Pew Research Center*. 22 Jun. 2016. Web. www.people-press.org/2016/06/22/partisanship-and-political-animosity-in-2016/
    Also, "Political Polarization in the American Public." *Pew Research Center*. 12 Jun. 2014. Web. www.people-press.org/2014/06/12/political-polarization-in-the-american-public/

35. Mutz, Diana C. "How the Mass Media Divide Us." In D. Brady and P. Divola (Eds.), *Red and Blue Nation*. Washington, DC: Brookings Institution Press, 2006. 223–48. Web. http://repository.upenn.edu/asc_papers/126

36. Mitchell, Amy, Jeffrey Gottfriend, Michael Barthel, and Elisa Shearer. "How Americans Get Their News: Pathways to News." *Pew Research Center*. 7 Jul. 2016. Web. www.journalism.org/2016/07/07/pathways-to-news/

37. Hwang, Hyunseo, Youngju Kim, and Catherine U. Huh. "Seeing Is Believing: Effects of Uncivil Online Debate on Political Polarization and Expectations of Deliberation." *Journal of Broadcasting & Electronic Media*. 2014. Volume 58, Issue 4. Web. http://dx.doi.org/10.1080/08838151.2014.966365

38. Anderson, Ashley A., Dominique Brossard, Dietram A. Scheufele, Michael A. Xenos, and Peter Ladwig. "The 'Nasty Effect': Online Incivility and Risk Perceptions of Emerging Technologies." *Journal of Computer Mediated Communication*. 19 Feb. 2013. Volume 19, Issue 3. Web. http://dx.doi.org/10.1111/jcc4.12009

39. Talk of the Nation, NPR. "The 'Nasty Effect': How Comments Color Comprehension." *NPR*. 11 Mar. 2013. Web. www.npr.org/2013/03/11/174027294/the-nasty-effect-how-comments-color-comprehension

40. Lee, Eun-Ju. "That's Not the Way It Is: How User-Generated Comments on the News Affect Perceived Media Bias." *Journal of Computer Mediated Communication* 18 (10 Oct. 2012): 32–45. Web. http://onlinelibrary.wiley.com/doi/10.1111/j.1083-6101.2012.01597.x/abstract
    Also, Rolston, Dorian. "Online Story Comments Affect News Perception." *Columbia Journalism Review*. 14 Dec. 2012. Web. http://archives.cjr.org/behind_the_news/comments_color_news_perception.php

41. Stray, Jonathan. "How Do You Tell When the News Is Biased? It Depends on How You See Yourself." *Nieman Lab*. 27 Jun. 2012. Web. www.niemanlab.org/2012/06/how-do-you-tell-when-the-news-is-biased/

42. Lanosga, Gerry, Damian Radcliffe, Frank Waddell, Glenn Scott, and Jennifer Glover Konfrst. "Experts' Roundtable: The Future of Journalism in Trump's America." *The Conversation*. 29 Nov. 2016. Web. https://theconversation.com/experts-roundtable-the-future-of-journalism-in-trumps-america-69545

43. Buckels, Erin E., Paul D. Trapnell, and Delroy L. Paulhus. "Trolls Just Want to Have Fun." *Personality and Individual Differences*. Sept. 2014. Volume 67. Web. www.sciencedirect.com/science/article/pii/S0191886914000324

44. "Online Harassment, Digital Abuse and Cyberstalking in America." *Data & Society Research Institute*. Nov. 2016. Web. www.datasociety.net/pubs/oh/Online_Harassment_2016.pdf

45. Moran, Kevin. "Journal Bids Farewell to Online Comments." *Manchester Journal*. New England Newspapers Inc. 23 Sept. 2016. Web. www.manchesterjournal.com/stories/journal-bids-farewell-to-online-comments,9425. New England Newspapers, Inc. includes *The Berkshire Eagle* (Pittsfield, MA); Bennington, *Banner* (Bennington, VT), Brattleboro, *Reformer* (Brattleboro, VT) and *Manchester Journal* (Manchester, VT)

46. McGaffey, Ruth. "The Heckler's Veto," *Marquette Law Review* 57 (1973): 1. Print.

47. Moran. "Journal Bids Farewell to Online Comments."

48. Santana, Arthur D. "Virtuous or Vitriolic." *Journalism Practice*. 18 Jul. 2013. Volume 8, Issue 1. Web. www.tandfonline.com/doi/abs/10.1080/17512786.2013.813194

49. Corcoran, Lindsay. "Negative News Media, Internet 'Trolling' Making Worcester Residents Fearful." *Masslive.com*, 22 Jun. 2015. Web. www.masslive.com/news/worcester/index.ssf/2015/06/negative_news_media_internet_t.html

50. Dewey, Caitlin. "The Only Guide to Gamergate You Will Ever Need to Read." *The Washington Post*. 14 Oct. 2014. Web. www.washingtonpost.com/news/the-intersect/wp/2014/10/14/the-only-guide-to-gamergate-you-will-ever-need-to-read

51. VanDerWerff, Todd. "Why Is Everybody in the Video Game World Fighting? #Gamergate." *Vox*. 6 Sept. 2014. Web. www.vox.com/2014/9/6/6111065/gamergate-explained-everybody-fighting

52. Pierson, Emma. "Outnumbered but Well-Spoken: Female Commenters in the New York Times." *In Proceedings of the 18th ACM Conference on Computer Supported Cooperative Work & Social Computing*. New York, NY: ACM. 2015. Web. http://cs.stanford.edu/people/emmap1/cscw_paper.pdf

53. Martin, Fiona. "Getting My Two Cents Worth in: Access, Interaction, Participation and Social Inclusion in Online News Commenting." *ISOJ Journal*. Spring 2016. Volume 6, Issue 1. Web. https://isojjournal.wordpress.com/2015/04/15/getting-my-two-cents-worth-in-access-interaction-participation-and-social-inclusion-in-online-news-commenting/

54. Stroud, Van Duyn, Alizor, and Lang. "News Commenters and News Comment Readers."

55. Ibid.

56. Nielsen, Jakob. "The 90–9–1 Rule for Participation Inequality in Social Media and Online Communities." *Nielsen Norman Group*. 9 Oct. 2006. Web. www.nngroup.com/articles/participation-inequality

57. Nielsen, Jakob. "Community Is Dead; Long Live Mega-Collaboration." Nielsen Norman Group. 15 Aug. 1997. Web. www.nngroup.com/articles/community-is-dead-long-live-mega-collaboration

58. Nielsen. "The 90–9–1 Rule for Participation Inequality in Social Media and Online Communities."

59. "The State of Community Management 2016." The Community Roundtable. 17 May 2016. Web. www.communityroundtable.com/research/the-state-of-community-management/socm2016/

60. Jensen, Elizabeth. "NPR Website to Get Rid of Comments." *NPR*. 17 Aug. 2016. Web. www.npr.org/sections/ombudsman/2016/08/17/489516952/npr-website-to-get-rid-of-comments

61. Zamora, Amanda. "Comments Are Changing: Our Commitment to Audiences Shouldn't." *Poynter Institute*. 31 Aug. 2016. Web. www.poynter.org/2016/comments-are-changing-our-commitment-to-audiences-shouldnt/428399

62. Franklin, Brad. "Online Comments to Stories Vile and Hateful." *The Clarion-Ledger*. 15 Dec. 2015. Web. www.clarionledger.com/story/opinion/columnists/2015/12/14/franklin-online-comments-stories-vile-and-hateful/77325286/

63. Reid, Alastair. "How Are Journalists at Risk of Vicarious Trauma from UGC?" *Journalism.co.uk*. 13 Oct. 2014. Web. www.journalism.co.uk/news/how-are-journalists-at-risk-of-vicarious-trauma-from-ugc-/s2/a562758/

64. Hermida. *Tell Everyone: Why We Share & Why It Matters*.

65. Rost, Katja, Lea Stahel, and Bruno S. Frey. "Digital Social Norm Enforcement: Online Firestorms in Social Media." *PLoS One*. Public Library of Science. 17 Jun. 2016. Web. http://journals.plos.org/plosone/article?id=10.1371%2Fjournal.pone.0155923

66. Valenti, Jessica. "Not All Comments Are Created Equal: The Case for Ending Online Comments." *The Guardian*. 10 Sept. 2015. Web. www.theguardian.com/commentisfree/2015/sep/10/end-online-comments

67. "We Have a Rape Gif Problem and Gawker Media Won't Do Anything About It." *Jezebel*. Gawker Media, 11 Aug. 2014. Web. http://jezebel.com/we-have-a-rape-gif-problem-and-gawker-media-wont-do-any-1619384265/all

68. Gardiner, Becky, Mahana Mansfield, Ian Anderson, Josh Holder, Daan Louter, and Monica Ulmanu. "The Dark Side of Guardian Comments." *The Guardian*. 12 Apr. 2016. Web. www.theguardian.com/technology/2016/apr/12/the-dark-side-of-guardian-comments

69. Ubiñas, Helen. Email interview. 6 Jun. 2017.

70. Ibid.

71. "Public Safety Information on Swatting." National 911 Program. National Highway Traffic Safety Administration's Office of Emergency Medical Services. 911.gov. May 2015. Web. www.911.gov/pdf/PublicSafetyInfo-Swatting-may2015.pdf

72. Ubinas. Email interview.

73. Ibid.

74. Ziegele, Marc, and Oliver Quiring. "Conceptualizing Online Discussion Value: A Multidimensional Framework for Analyzing User Comments on Mass-Media Websites." *Annals of the International Communication Association*. 2013. Volume 37, Issue 1. Web. http://dx.doi.org/10.1080/23808985.2013.11679148

75. Herbst, Susan. *Rude Democracy: Civility and Incivility in American Politics*. Philadelphia, PA: Temple University Press, 2010. Print.

76. Cheng, J., M. Bernstein, C. Danescu-Niculescu-Mizil, and J. Leskovec. "Anyone Can Become a Troll: Causes of Trolling Behavior in Online Discussions." In *Proceedings of the 2017 ACM Conference on Computer Supported Cooperative Work and Social Computing*. ACM, New York, NY. 2017. Web. https://doi.org/10.1145/2998181.2998213

77. Kubota, Taylor. "Yes, Anyone Can Become an Internet Troll." *Stanford University News*. 8 Feb. 2017. Web. http://news.stanford.edu/2017/02/06/stanford-research-shows-anyone-can-become-internet-troll/

78. Dahlgren, Peter. "The Internet, Public Spheres, and Political Communication: Dispersion and Deliberation." *Political Communication.* 2005. Volume 22, Issue 2. Web. http://dx.doi.org/10.1080/10584600590933160

79. Citron, Danielle Keats, and Helen L. Norton. "Intermediaries and Hate Speech: Fostering Digital Citizenship for Our Information Age." *Boston University Law Review.* 2011. Volume 91, 1435; University of Maryland Legal Studies Research Paper No. 2011–16. Web. https://papers.ssrn.com/sol3/papers.cfm?abstract_id=1764004

80. Ibid.

81. Ibid.

82. Santana, Arthur D. "Controlling the Conversation: The Availability of Commenting Forums in Online Newspapers." *Journalism Studies.* 31 Oct. 2014. Volume 17, Issue 2. Web. http://dx.doi.org/10.1080/1461670X.2014.972076

83. Ward, Stephen J. A. "A 'Right to Offend' Should Be Balanced by a 'Duty to Mend'." *MediaShift.* 25 Feb. 2015. Web. http://mediashift.org/2015/02/a-right-to-offend-should-be-balanced-by-a-duty-to-mend/

84. Williams, Juan. "Why I Blame the GOP for Civility's Breakdown." *FOX News.* 19 Jan. 2017. Web. www.foxnews.com/opinion/2016/01/19/why-blame-gop-for-civilitys-breakdown.html

85. Shanahan. "How News Sites' Online Comments Helped Build Our Hateful Electorate."

86. Horowitz, Rick. "The [Minority Writers] Seminar: What, How, Why." Association of Opinion Journalists archive. 23 Sept. 2014. Web. http://asne.org/content.asp?contentid=468

5   Contradictions of Anonymity

> My mood, I say, was one of exaltation. I felt as a seeing man might do, with
> padded feet and noiseless clothes, in a city of the blind. I experienced a wild
> impulse to jest, to startle people, to clap men on the back, fling people's hats
> astray, and generally revel in my extraordinary advantage.
> —H. G. Wells, *The Invisible Man*, Chapter 21[1]

An anonymous online comment posted at the bottom of a local politics story
set off a journalistic quandary at *The Salt Lake Tribune* in July 2015. The
comment, submitted by a user with the screen name WhiskeyPete, slammed
the quality of the Utah newspaper's political reporting. A reader flagged
the post as "objectionable." Although the criticism was harsh, the comment
itself was on topic and didn't use abusive or defamatory language. A newsroom web producer reviewed the flagged submission based on *sltrib.com*'s
online commenting policy, deemed it appropriate and left it in public view.[2]

But because WhiskeyPete's posting had been flagged by a reader, the
Tribune's online comment management system—a popular third platform
called Disqus[3]—displayed to the web producer the email address Whiskey-
Pete used to register on *sltrib.com*. That's when the web producer noticed
something unexpected. WhiskeyPete's registration email address contained
the same name as the city mayor's official spokesperson: Art Raymond.[4]

If WhiskeyPete was actually the Salt Lake City mayor's spokesperson,
what other comments might he have posted surreptitiously on *Tribune*
news stories about his boss or his boss's political rivals? The web producer performed a search of WhiskeyPete's submission history on Disqus.
The archive revealed numerous comments by WhiskeyPete on *Tribune*
news stories and on another local politics site, *UtahPolicy.com*.[5] Combing
through the contributions, *Tribune* news staff identified six questionable
WhiskeyPete posts on five *Tribune* articles that either expressed support
for the mayor or lobbed potshots at the mayor's opponents in an upcoming

primary election. The time stamps on those six comments also revealed they had been posted during city business hours and originated from a computer with a city-owned internet protocol (IP) address.[6]

When reporters at the *Tribune* confronted Raymond with their findings, he acknowledged writing the comments under the WhiskeyPete pseudonym from the computer in his city hall office.[7] Raymond argued he had the "right as guaranteed under the First Amendment to have a personal opinion" about what was going on in the city where he resides.[8] Raymond said he posted the remarks during his work breaks, writing them in a personal capacity, and that no other city employee had asked him to write them or knew he was composing them.

However, as a public employee, Raymond's covert online communiqués during city business hours on the website of Utah's largest newspaper raised ethical and legal alarms. His online comments—no longer anonymous to the *Tribune* news staff—could be construed as illegal campaigning. By journalistic standards, Raymond's anonymous online activity was now newsworthy and warranted news coverage in the public's interest.

Yet a key ingredient of this unexpectedly newsworthy story—perhaps even the catalyst for it—was the *Tribune*'s website, its online commenting system and its online commenting policy. If the *Tribune* had not allowed anonymity in its comments section, would Raymond have felt so comfortable publicly sharing his opinions there?

The unusual situation raised a host of other questions for news organizations that allow anonymous or pseudonymous user participation. Does the facade of digital anonymity lure and encourage people to engage in riskier speech, which news organizations can then turn into stories? If a system of online participation permits users to hide their real names, does a news site imply a promise of anonymity to its contributors? Does a news site violate its own online privacy policy by publicly revealing the offline identity of a contributor? Is it ethical for newsroom editorial personnel to have access to the email and IP addresses of registered web users and/or subscribers—data typically collected by a news organization's business side? Is it in the public interest to even allow people to comment without their names attached?

Ultimately, the *Tribune* did publish news stories about the anonymous online postings of a city official who happened to be one of its online commenters and publicly stripped WhiskeyPete of his cyberanonymity in the process.[9] In doing so, the Utah news outlet joined a shortlist of online news organizations that have grappled with the controversial practice of permitting anonymous comments and then unmasking the writers in the public interest.

Anonymous online comments on news websites are a thorny digital outgrowth of journalism's long-established and often questionable use of unnamed sources. The "anonymous" part of public digital discourse has opened up a rabbit hole of contradictions for news sites that supply online forums for audience participation.

Anonymity refers to a social state of being in which a person is not identifiable.[10] An audience, especially a large news audience, plays a key role in this scenario, as anonymity is only achieved with the presence of an audience. On the internet, anonymity is an assembly of different levels of online "un-identifiability." This includes nondisclosure of personal information, lack of visibility and the absence of eye contact. Sites allow for completely anonymous input, such as Gawker's Kinja system, or they require some identifiability via email registration and a username and options to add avatar photos or other descriptive details. Anonymity therefore is concerned with the design structure of the medium, as well as individual and audience perceptions about the degree of anonymity afforded.[11] In the digital realm, these components can combine in different ways, yielding users a variety of "anonymities."[12]

Anonymity plays a role in both online discourse and journalism. When those roles muddled on the internet, incongruity followed. Many journalists blame anonymity for the incivility that overruns public discourse in online comment sections. Pulitzer Prize–winning columnist Leonard Pitts Jr. called anonymous online forums "havens for a level of crudity, bigotry, meanness and plain nastiness that shocks the tattered remnants of our propriety" and inspires many "to vent their most reptilian thoughts."[13] Journalism ethicist Robert McKay Steele observed, "With no name attached, the commenters basically wear a hood and swing a sharp axe."[14] Syndicated columnist Froma Harrop argued, "Web anonymity is often a force for evil in the civic conversation. . . . As for the sweaty mobs of posters going incognito as they drop poison on others, they are simply gutless."[15]

Yet the granting of "invisible attribution" to news sources is embedded in the history and culture of American journalism. "Journalists know that some stories that the public should see could not be published if the sources had to give their real names because of the wreckage the sources could face in their careers or lives," explained Kyle A. Heatherly, Anthony L. Fargo and Jason A. Martin in an International Press Institute report on anonymous commenting.[16] "Likewise, allowing people to comment anonymously or pseudonymously opens up forums for commentary and news tips to people who may fear negative consequences from peers, employers, or government officials."

Unnamed sources have contributed to some of journalism's greatest triumphs, such as *The Washington Post*'s reporting on the Watergate scandal.[17] Nameless informants have also fueled some of journalism's biggest failures, such as *The New York Times*'s reporting on supposed weapons of mass destruction in Iraq that swayed public opinion in favor of the Iraq war.[18]

"Anonymity is not an unusual condition sources place on their information, but a regular and often repeated practice," particularly in the national affairs reporting of elite news outlets, wrote Matt Carlson in his book *On the Condition of Anonymity*, which traces the history of journalism's use of anonymous news sources.[19] According to Carlson, journalists express a can't-live-with-them, can't-live-without-them dilemma with nameless attribution as the driving force behind public-interest news stories. Anonymity agreements with news sources are intended to be mutually beneficial. Journalists strike deals to keep identities secret in exchange for access to exclusive information. Sources gain wider awareness for their information and opinions, while journalists and their news organizations get a "scoop" and the attention that goes with an "exclusive" story.

By employing a system of unsigned digital commentary, news sites may attract and collect information from the public they would not obtain otherwise, such as the masked opinions of a public official in Salt Lake City.

Journalists can have other motivations to participate in a system of unnamed sources. Anonymous "official" sources can make a journalist seem more enterprising and connected. A news story may also be viewed by the public as more important if it includes prominent yet anonymous sources, Carlson argues.[20] However, both the news outlet and the journalist incur serious risk when the source or the online commenter who speaks without accountability turns out to be incorrect or deceitful, and thus not worthy of having been included in the professional news report.[21] "The opacity of unnamed sources also prevents audiences from gaining additional information from which to make judgments about unattributed information," Carlson explained.[22] If the public doesn't know the source's name, they can't google it for more information. In the previous chapter, we discussed the information distortion and poor news comprehension that can occur from caustic, unscrupulous and usually anonymous online comments.

Anonymity in news reporting and online news comments is in many ways a trap. Promises of anonymity may marshal honest responses from reticent sources who have safety and privacy concerns, but anonymity can also be exploited by self-serving sources for gamesmanship—meaning "the practice of winning a game or contest by doing things that seem unfair but that are not actually."[23] Sources given invisibility by journalists can manipulate the news in an individually beneficial way "rather than in a way that provides a social benefit."[24]

Journalists are trained to be on guard for sources who demand anonymity with intentions to use the press as a megaphone or to disparage enemies without accountability.[25] Anytime a news organization allows anonymous sources in reporting or online comments, the news outlet risks facilitating a flow of unattributed and unverifiable claims into the news. While anonymity can unearth useful information that supports the watchdog function of the press, it simultaneously undermines that same function through gratuitous application, Carlson warned. "When introducing an unnamed source into a news story, a journalist implies the value gained in making hidden information public outweighs the lack of transparency in withholding the source's identity."[26] Similar credibility concerns come into play when digital news outlets host anonymous online forums.

"Media outlet practices vary, but journalists should not overlook the danger of legal problems and credibility damage from publishing anonymously sourced information that is not confirmed by public records or credible sources," states an ethics paper on anonymous sourcing by Michael Farrell for the Society of Professional Journalists. "Before journalists allow themselves to be used by an anonymous source, they should be sure to question whether the news value warrants whatever the source hopes to accomplish."[27]

The frequent and sometimes unnecessary use of anonymous sources in news reporting can represent a "pattern of privileging sources above audiences," Carlson argues. Online anonymity for commenters in news site forums privileges unidentified commenters over the audience, as well. On news sites with unmoderated feedback forums, comment anonymity can give undue advantage to the most nefarious participants. There are commenters, better known as trolls, who exploit online anonymity for propaganda, disruption, personal revenge and "spreading misinformation or opinions without reprisal.[28]"

A psychological study of internet anonymity by Erin Buckels, Paul Trapnell and Delroy Paulhus suggests anonymity is especially attractive to people with a "dark triad" of characteristics. Individuals who are narcissistic, psychopathic and sadistic, who take pleasure in making others suffer, are more likely to leverage online anonymity as a means to an end.[29]

Because the laws surrounding online anonymity are in flux around the world, and because allowing readers and viewers to comment anonymously on stories raises ethical issues, many news outlets have proactively developed self-regulatory policies on whether to accept and how to manage anonymous comments on their sites, noted Heatherly, Fargo and Martin.[30] The inconsistency of those policies reflects the unsettled question of whether anonymity helps or hinders the practice and function of journalism.

A 2014 study by digital media researcher Arthur D. Santana found that nearly half (48.9%) of the 137 largest newspaper websites in the United States had stopped allowing anonymous comments. Meanwhile, about 42% of those newspaper sites continued to provide anonymity to commenters.[31] Santana's study also revealed that just under a tenth of U.S. newspapers (9.4%) did not offer any on-site commenting forums at all.

Another survey of 101 online news publishers by the Associated Press Media Editors Association in 2014 determined that 94% provided online comment sections. Many respondents said they believed allowing comments was important to encourage community discussions in a public forum. The survey showed 46% of those sites permitted anonymity. However, the majority (54%) required commenters to identify themselves in some way, and 38% went so far as to require first and last names.[32]

Anonymous online comments have fallen out of favor among a majority of news sites. "That particular retrenchment of access has snowballed since 2010, driven largely by anecdotal and unsubstantiated claims that anonymous online forums had 'scared off' some readers," argued digital media researcher Bill Reader. "More accurately, the tone of unregulated discourse often offended the sensibilities of the control-obsessed media elites, many of them still pining for the 'good old days' of 20th-century style gatekeeping."

Reader criticized the journalism industry for "relying on gut-reactions to extreme examples" and ignoring the fact that anonymous forums also include "multiple expressions of opinion that are polite, reasoned, informed, and sincere. They just come from people who, for whatever reason, are not comfortable writing more traditional, signed letters to the editor."[33]

Privacy, Safety and Consequence-Free Speech

> Sometimes the truth is uttered from behind a mask; banning the mask may also ban the truth.
> —Kyle A. Heatherly, Anthony L. Fargo and Jason A. Martin[34]

Since anonymity and pseudonymity were standard attributes of online discourse in the early days of the internet, most news outlets adopted the same policy for their forums when commenting became a component of the digital news terrain in the late 1990s and early 2000s. The wild and wooly culture of the young internet placed a high value on independence, unfettered freedom of expression and anonymity. Human use of technology had undergone a revolution thanks to pervasive networking. Computers were no longer just tools to run calculations or to solve problems. The internet had become a means for externalizing the self in a vast digital landscape where a person's essence could be abstracted from their physical shell and roam free.[35]

Newsroom leaders recognized that the online audience of "netizens" would be reluctant to join in cybernews discussions without the same shield of anonymity they enjoyed elsewhere on the web, even if ethically, the anonymity raised red flags for journalists. Most comment systems on news sites were initially designed with a low threshold for participation with either no registration or very simple registration, usually just a valid email address and pseudonym for a username. Some digital discussion systems, such as Topix, even withheld the actual identity of commenters from news-room personnel.

Critical anonymous speech has propagated widely in cyberspace ever since, as evidenced by the popularity of web-based consumer rating services such as Yelp, Angie's List, TripAdvisor and Ratemyprofessor. A distinct culture of anonymous commenting grew out of both digital constraints and the relative absence of regulation.[36] Everyone and everything is subject to anonymous online review nowadays, from products on Amazon.com to auctioneers on eBay to rooms for rent on Airbnb.

Most Americans consider online anonymity an important component of the digital realm, according to multiple surveys conducted by the Pew Research Center. In 2013, at least 25% of internet users said they had posted material online without revealing who they are.[37] Another survey from the same year put the spotlight on people's concerns about online privacy, determining 86% of internet users had taken steps online to remove or mask their digital footprints. And more than half (55%) of internet users said they took the steps to avoid online observation by specific people, organizations or the government.[38]

A majority of adults (55%) agreed in a 2015 Pew survey that people should have the ability to use the internet completely anonymously for certain kinds of online activities, as long as the actions did not present a threat to others. Detailed responses to survey questions suggested many Americans continue to believe anonymity is essential to ensure freedom of expression. More than a quarter of adults remained "undecided" on the issue of online anonymity (27%), while 16% of adults were against it, findings showed.[39]

A survey by the audience engagement company LiveFyre in 2014 suggested if news sites removed the option of anonymous commenting, many audience members would stop participating in forums.[40] The company asked 1,300 users between the ages of 18 and 65 if they ever chose to comment anonymously and why. Most respondents said they disguised their identity because they didn't want their comments to negatively affect their business, employment or personal lives by being connected to their real names. They also used the shield of anonymity when they wanted attention to be focused on the ideas in their comments rather than their identity. Nearly 80% of those surveyed said if a site forced them to log in with their real name, they would not comment at all.

When *ESPN*, *The Dallas Morning News* and *The Hartford Courant* tied more accountability to user comments on their websites using social media authentication methods in 2013, the resulting comment drop-off was viewed by editors as a quality-over-quantity tradeoff.[41] Sites that require commenters to use their real identities typically make people sign in through a specific commenting system or link to a social network account like Facebook or Google. But tying together various online accounts and identities raises privacy alarms for some audience members. Other potential participants get turned off by the extra time and steps it takes to leave just one comment—blaming poor user experience.

Political scientists point out that despite democratic free speech protections, most of the citizenry does not participate in public discourse anyway. "Most people are not effectively motivated to get information, to form opinions, or to discuss issues with those who have different points of view. Each citizen has only one vote or voice in millions and most have other pressing demands on their time," James Fishkin observed.[42]

People also have legitimate reasons for self-censoring their public speech. Some feel they don't have anything to add to the discussion. Others think participation is pointless because they don't have access to policy makers, influencers or a substantial audience.[43] "The key to any deliberative microcosm is that it effectively motivates participants to engage with each other and with the issues," Fishkin argued. "Ordinarily most people do not have the time or inclination to become involved in politics or public policy partly because they do not believe their voice matters."

Some audience members worry about the monitoring of their public online activity by employers and the long-term (archival) impact of their public speech on their reputation. There are fears about online harassment and intimidation, especially if users have previously witnessed or experienced incivility and hostility in public discourse arenas. Self-censorship exacerbates participation inequality, as it keeps people from commenting publicly on news articles pertinent to their own communities.

Peer pressure is a factor, too. It can be risky to share thoughts in a public forum when it's also necessary to maintain relationships with others who don't share the same views or values. In situations in which users know posts will be visible to a primary network of colleagues, friends and family members, they may be less willing to share authentic opinions if they think their social network might disagree, causing a "spiral of silence."[44]

Publishing comments on news sites and social media channels does increase opportunities for ordinary citizens' speech to gain wider attention because material may be received by larger audiences. The option to engage in anonymous online speech can remove some fears of retribution. Anonymity has other advantages, too. It means the audience must evaluate the speaker's ideas based on words alone, observed Jason C. Miller.[45] Rather than the author's reputation coming first, anonymous work is judged on its own merit and, presumably, received with less bias. Anonymity disguises status indicators such as race, class, gender, ethnicity and age—elements that often allow elite speakers to dominate real-world discourse. Anonymity enables a diversity of viewpoints in cyberspace, especially on hot-button topics, such as abortion, religion and politics. Even so-called "bitch" sites may add something of value to the digital commons by making more information available, Miller argued.[46]

In addition, online anonymity offers a semblance of safety to members of marginalized groups who are more likely to endure hate speech, cyberbullying and harassment online, giving them room to engage in rhetoric in the public sphere. Studies show women are more likely to use anonymity online for protection from online harassment.[47]

Critics of real-name comment policies argue that eliminating anonymity to squelch trolling is a doubled-edged sword that prevents whistle blowing and the free exchange of ideas. By nature, online conversations are informal, mostly anonymous, spontaneous and controversial.[48] Without anonymity, certain audience members who cannot afford to be publicly known would find it impossible to comment, especially in online forums about politics, medical issues, sexuality or some other human condition that could cause them to be discriminated against. Research also shows requiring real names to be published with opinions in the United States correlates with forums being dominated by white, middle-class males who are generally better educated and more socioeconomically secure.[49]

Humans adapt their behavior to different environments, including online ones, depending on the structure, rules and consequences. Responsible news sites should try to curb incivility, bullying and trolling in public discourse areas, but proponents of anonymity would prefer better forum moderation, not taking away the freedom of the innocent or those who would be harmed by having their words connected to a real-life identity.[50]

"Most who traverse the Net likely have run into the vile, the profane, the distasteful speech that seems always to lurk just a few comments down on so many Web pages, regardless of the discussion or issue," explained Gene Policinski, senior vice president of the First Amendment Center. "Nothing in the 45 words of the First Amendment mandates tastefulness, political correctness or even that we identify ourselves when we speak to our fellow citizens."[51]

Journalism, in practice and as a profession, champions free speech. The First Amendment protects the right to anonymous speech. That right isn't absolute, but it does protect people who choose to remain anonymous when engaging in lawful speech. "People sometimes have extraordinarily good reasons for not wanting to be identified," observed journalism professor emeritus Wayne Worcester, one of my colleagues at the University of Connecticut. "You could argue that, well, their free speech is protected, so what's the problem? The problem is the First Amendment protects their free speech, but it doesn't offer them any blanket protection from retribution."[52]

Hardline journalism traditionalists may believe improving public discourse on news sites can happen only by imposing online news organizations with the same responsibilities the rest of conventional media employs, "but the problem with that," Worcester said, "is that greater responsibility and an enforced higher regard for untainted fact seems likely to force a shrinkage of the internet to about the size of a hair net."[53]

Faceless, Nameless, Merciless

> You end up wanting to fight someone, kill them, or kill yourself—usually all three at once.
> —Eminem, on reading online comments[54]

The digital iteration of "anonymity" in news site comment sections is not equal to the anonymity reporters grant to news sources. During the newsgathering process, the real name, job title, age, location and/or biases of an anonymous news source are made known to the individual reporter and his or her editors before anonymity is granted. That is not usually the case with anonymous online commenters. Most print news outlets refuse to publish anonymous letters to the editor. Journalists have gone to jail defending the confidentiality of anonymous news sources. How many journalists would be willing to be imprisoned to protect an anonymous comment troll?

Many journalists argue allowing anonymous online comments is antithetical to professional journalism ethics. "Professional journalists only allow sources to be anonymous when there is no other way to get important information. That same ethic should apply to web comments," explained Eric Newton, innovation chief at the Walter Cronkite School of Journalism and Mass Communication.[55] Traditional news organizations made a "destructive mistake" by encouraging anonymous comments on their websites, Newton argued. "Letting your comment section turn into a sewer weakens the reputation of a newspaper or any other fact-based business."[56]

The Society of Professional Journalists code of ethics contains two direct statements on anonymous sources. The first advises journalists to "identify sources clearly. The public is entitled to as much information as possible to judge the reliability and motivations of sources." The second warns news purveyors to "consider sources' motives before promising anonymity. Reserve anonymity for sources who may face danger, retribution or other harm, and have information that cannot be obtained elsewhere. Explain why anonymity was granted."[57]

If news organizations intend to build bridges of free and open debate, they should be "structures of integrity—held together by facts, civil discussion, accountability, constructive and useful comments," Newton asserted. "What's the point of having a code of ethics if journalists ignore it?"[58]

There are some audience members who use anonymity in comment sections as the internet-age equivalent of a heavy-breathing, random crank call. But more harmful motives for communication without attribution include intimidation, insulation, concealment, crime or fraud.[59] Anonymous sources and their online commenting counterparts often provide erroneous information to news outlets "because why make sure you have it right when you will not be held accountable for what you say?" observed John Christie, cofounder of the Maine Center for Public Interest Reporting. "Many sources hide behind anonymity to take cheap shots without anyone knowing they have an axe to grind or a dog in the fight."[60]

Two assumptions fuel the anti-anonymity movement in the digital space. First, that the irresistible corruption of anonymity breeds negativity. Psychologist John Suler's toxic online disinhibition theory, which we discussed in Chapter 3, supports this idea. No monitors, minimized authority, personal invisibility and low risk of consequences enable a greater openness in online speakers and encourages misbehavior, Suler theorized.[61] Anonymity can cause internet users to feel unaccountable for negative actions, as they cannot be identified as the perpetrators, thus increasing their levels of toxic disinhibition. Anonymity and the impersonal nature of computer-mediated conversations provide the chance to defy social norms, triggering more impulsive behaviors.

Anonymity within widely distributed news reports has on occasion become a "forum for elite sources," such as high-level government officials, to talk to each other, Carlson observed.[62] In the online space, some anonymous forums serve as covert gathering spaces for gangs of trolls, propagandists and terrorists. "The anonymity provided by the internet fosters communities where people can feed on each other's hate without consequence. They can easily form into mobs and terrify victims," wrote Adrian Chen in an *MIT Technology Review* article about trolls. "Individual trolls can hide behind dozens of screen names to multiply their effect. And attempts to curb online hate must always contend with the long-standing ideals that imagine the internet's main purpose as offering unfettered space for free speech and marginalized ideas."[63]

In 2014, digital media researcher Santana analyzed 900 randomly chosen user comments on articles about immigration. Half of the comments originated from news sites with anonymous postings, and half came from sites that did not offer anonymity. Santana's study confirmed the theory that anonymous comments tend to be less civil. Results showed more than half

(53%) of the anonymous speakers posted uncivil comments. The level of incivility dropped to 29% when real names or links to Facebook accounts were required.[64]

Another experiment by Noam Lapidot-Lefler and Azy Barak looked at anonymity, invisibility and the lack of eye contact—the three main contributors to online disinhibition. The researchers found lack of eye contact to be the chief culprit for the negative effects of online disinhibition, concluding the sense of "un-identifiability" factors strongly in how people behave badly online.[65]

Online gamers popularized their own theory about anonymity in the digital space. Known as "John Gabriel's Greater Internet Fuckwad Theory," the concept originated with a March 2004 *Penny Arcade* webcomic by Mike Krahulik and Jerry Holkins. The theory asserts when a normal person is given anonymity and a captive audience on the internet, they lose social inhibitions and act like a jerk.[66]

Reaching back to the fourth century, Plato also provides an anonymity thought experiment in the story of the Ring of Gyges. Plato's parable about human self-control and corruption is told by the character Glaucon, a student of Socrates, who disputes his teacher's position that all men want to be moral because they recognize justice and virtue are desirable in themselves.[67]

Glaucon describes Gyges as just a lowly shepherd of the king's flock, when one day a great earthquake opened up a hole in the earth in front of him. Gyges descended into the hole and discovered a hollow bronze horse with doors. Inside the doors lay a dead body with a gold ring on its finger. Gyges takes the ring and wears it to the next meeting of the shepherds. While sitting among his colleagues and fiddling with the ring, Gyges realizes when he turns it backwards, he is invisible. Since one of the shepherds must go to the king's court to give a report, Gyges recognizes an opportunity to exploit his invisibility and volunteers to visit the king. At court, Gyges seduces the queen, kills the king and steals the crown. Glaucon argues this is what all men would do if they could get away with it. Anyone with such a ring of invisibility would be a fool not to do what Gyges did, Glaucon explains, concluding, "a man is just, not willingly or because he thinks that justice is any good to him individually, but of necessity, for wherever anyone thinks that he can safely be unjust, there he is unjust."[68]

The second assumption that drives the anti-anonymity movement is the belief that unsigned comments shape the opinions and behaviors of those who encounter them. In the previous chapter, we explored "the hostile media effect"—in which user comments raise the audience's suspicions of media bias[69]—and "the nasty effect"—in which uncivil comments cause readers to become polarized about the contents of a news article.[70] Another experiment by journalism professors Kevin Wallsten and Melinda Tarsi measured whether anonymous comments affect people's attitudes toward the news media. The researchers exposed study participants to varying amounts of media criticism in an anonymous comments section attached to a hypothetical *USA Today* news story. Their findings showed participants becoming significantly more negative toward the news media in general and *USA Today* in particular when exposed to a story with an anonymous comments section. The negativity lingered even when the anonymous comments praised the news media's reporting. Wallsten and Tarsi concluded exposure to anonymous comments—regardless of their tone—leads internet users to dislike specific news organizations and the media in general.[71]

The mistrust readers already hold for the news media can be reinforced when journalists use anonymous sources in news reports. Even if the information is accurate, "readers cannot judge the value of the material for themselves if they don't know the source," noted Christie of the Maine Center for Public Interest Reporting. "They don't know who is speaking so they can't trust it; they can't tell if it is real or made up; they can't tell if the source has an agenda or is even knowledgeable."[72] Anonymous online commentary below a reported news story can have the same effect, as studies show comments in general undermine facts and warp understanding.[73]

Because anonymity reduces people's awareness of others, it can also affect the expression and interpretation of comments made during a digital discussion. A study by Russell Haines, Jill Hough, Lan Cao and Douglas Haines found that anonymity bolsters contrarians. Nameless comments led to more arguments in support of questionable behavior that was contrary to the majority opinion while at the same time decreasing the influence of other contrary arguments.[74] The researchers also witnessed less change in users' opinions under conditions of anonymity than when those commenting were identified. If changing minds is a goal of public digital discourse, anonymous speakers are not as effective as identifiable ones.[75]

Protecting Anonymous Speech

> On the internet, nobody knows you're a dog.
> —Peter Steiner, 1993 *New Yorker* cartoon[76]

American courts do not take lightly to unmasking anonymous speech. The U.S. Supreme Court has repeatedly ruled that anonymous speech is permitted and protected by the First Amendment. The highly cited 1995 Supreme Court ruling in *McIntyre v. Ohio Elections Commission* states,

> Protections for anonymous speech are vital to democratic discourse. Allowing dissenters to shield their identities frees them to express

critical, minority views. . . . Anonymity is a shield from the tyranny of the majority. . . . It thus exemplifies the purpose behind the Bill of Rights, and of the First Amendment in particular: to protect unpopular individuals from retaliation . . . at the hand of an intolerant society.[77]

Another key federal case dealing with anonymous speech on the internet, *Doe v. 2TheMart.com, Inc. (2001)*, echoed the Supreme Court's earlier sentiments.

> Anonymous speech is a great tradition that is woven into the fabric of this nation's history. The right to speak anonymously extends to speech via the internet. Internet anonymity facilitates the rich, diverse, and far ranging exchange of ideas. . . . People who have committed no wrongdoing should be free to participate in online forums without fear that their identity will be exposed under the authority of the court.

Yet no lawmaker, even those of the late-20th century, could have predicted how humans would come to use networked communication technology in 2017 and beyond. Any website that provides an open place for discussion and user-generated content can inadvertently enable calumny. And anonymous online publishing systems have fomented some truly abhorrent behavior. Take, for example, the case of Michael Brutsch, a prolifically offensive user of the social discussion platform Reddit who was labeled as one of the "biggest trolls on the web" in 2012.[78] Hiding behind the pseudonym "Violentacrez," Brutsch regularly used Reddit's open publishing system to create hundreds of discussion subforums dedicated to topics like "Rapebait," "Incest," "Pics of Dead Kids," "Choke a Bitch" and "Rape Jokes." Brutsch was accused of posting sexualized images of underage girls and graphic images of domestic violence.[79]

It was journalist Adrian Chen who outed Brutsch's real-life identity in a *Gawker* news article. After being unmasked, Brutsch blamed Reddit for breeding and feeding his knack for attracting a crowd and eliciting "discussion" about abominable subjects. Reddit's online system at the time rewarded forum creators and moderators for generating page views and audience participation, indiscriminate of the subject matter.[80]

Publicity surrounding repugnant incidents of anonymous online speech puts pressure on websites to clean house. Reddit has since become more heavy-handed with banning toxic "subreddit" forums.[81] But all internet service providers, including news sites, still enjoy legal protection from civil or criminal liability from user comments under Section 230 of the Communications Decency Act of 1996. The federal law immunizes website operators from responsibility for potentially damaging content others may post on their sites.

When first enacted by Congress, Section 230 was intended to foster openness and innovation on the World Wide Web by giving websites broad legal protections and allowing the internet to grow as a true marketplace of ideas. Advocates of online free speech at the time had argued that if controls were as tight on internet communication as with offline communication, the constant threat of litigation would intimidate individuals from weighing in on important issues of public concern. The provision states, "No provider of an interactive computer service shall be treated as a publisher of any information provided by a third party."[82] Section 230 defines an "interactive computer service" as "any information service, system, or access software provider that provides or enables computer access by multiple users to a computer server." An "information content provider" is considered "any person or entity that is responsible, in whole or in part, for the creation or development of information provided through the internet or any other interactive computer service."[83]

Most online news outlets are considered both "content providers" and "service providers." News sites provide content in the original stories, photographs and videos that paid staff and freelancers produce and post under the auspices of editorial supervision. They are also "service providers" to the extent that news sites allow audience members to add material to the organization's website through comments, blog posts, emailed news tips and automated headline feeds.

Section 230 ensures that those who host rather than author speech on the internet cannot be treated, for legal purposes, as having published it. Prior to the law's passage in 1996, website operators were afraid to touch anything posted by users for fear of being deemed "editors" or "publishers" of the material and therefore incurring liability.[84] Section 230 immunity does allow search engines and news websites to make modest edits to user contributions without fearing liability.[85] A site will lose the protection of Section 230, though, if in editing the content or phrasing of a user contribution, the information becomes defamatory.[86]

The shield of Section 230 prevents frivolous suits from being brought against online service providers, but the immunity does not extend to the originator of the online speech. People are liable for their own postings and comments anywhere on the web, whether published anonymously or not.

Because of the quantity of user-generated content and how quickly it is shared online, lawmakers recognized the hardship web intermediaries would face if they had to check and edit all user-generated material in the same way traditional publishers review submitted content. Meanwhile, traditional offline information providers—such as newspapers, book and magazine publishers and broadcast media outlets—continue to be held liable if they publish or distribute defamatory material. The inconsistency exasperates critics of Section 230, who say online publishers benefit from more protection than offline publishers, and the advantage online publishers enjoy under Section 230 helped web publishers grow while their traditional print and broadcast counterparts declined.

As the information landscape evolves, outdated distinctions between digital and traditional publishers may elicit changes.[87] Access and use of the internet is far more widespread in 2017 than it was in 1996. Social networking services like Facebook and Twitter did not exist in 1996. The reach of traditional print and broadcast media has weakened. A defamatory, anonymous statement made on the internet in 2017 will likely cause the same, if not more, harm than a similar statement made in a traditional information service because the number of people who can potentially access the statement is now greater online.

Although news sites that host anonymous or pseudonymous digital forums are protected by Section 230 from comment liability, online news purveyors can still be pulled into litigation through discovery subpoenas from aggrieved persons, businesses and organizations that wish to unmask the anonymous authors of defamatory comments or the anonymous violators of copyright laws.

State and federal courts have struggled to balance the First Amendment rights of free speech and freedom of the press—including anonymous speech—against the statutory and common-law protections accorded to those who genuinely believe their reputations are being seriously—and all too readily—damaged by falsehoods posted publicly in cyberspace. Courts have waded into anonymous comments on news sites and occasionally ruled to force a news organization to unmask a commenter. In July 2010, for example, a three-judge panel of the Appellate Court of Illinois ordered the Ottawa Publishing Company to turn over the email address of an anonymous commenter named FabFive to the attorney representing Donald and Janet Maxon of Ottawa.[88] Two years earlier, the Maxons had embarked on a legal fight to unmask a commenter with the pseudonym FabFive, whose comments on *MyWebTimes.com* accused the Maxons of bribing members of the Ottawa Plan Commission to establish a bed-and-breakfast business at their home.[89]

A coalition of advocacy and news organizations banded together to help fight the lawsuit, including Gannett Company, Hearst Corporation, Illinois Press Association, Online News Association, Online Publishers Association, Reporters Committee for Freedom of the Press and Tribune Company.[90] The coalition threw their support behind the right of anonymous online speech in a friend-of-the-court brief, arguing "Should the courts deprive internet speakers of their anonymity without appropriate safeguards, the uninhibited and robust exchange of ideas that has sprung up on news web sites will be chilled."[91]

The Illinois Appellate Court still concluded otherwise. The court's decision stated, "The statements that the Maxons bribed certain officials in order to obtain approval for their zoning request are not mere statements of opinion. . . . We find that the statements purport to be factual allegations of bribery by the Maxons and must be answered."[92] The ruling signaled a warning to online news organizations. News sites with anonymous commenting could expect more aggrieved individuals and businesses to file "John Doe" lawsuits to unmask the unnamed critics publishing in news sites' comment sections.

Journalism's Unmasking Prerogative

While the U.S. Supreme Court has ruled that government entities cannot prohibit anonymity as a condition for public speech, it does not mean citizens have an inalienable right to post anonymously in privately owned online forums. There is nothing to prohibit any non-government website from requiring users to identify themselves. There is also no law that prevents a non-government website from revealing the identity of an anonymous online commenter. Public opinion, however, can be a different story. When the *Salt Lake Tribune* publicly unmasked WhiskeyPete as Raymond, the Utah news outlet was blasted for betraying the trust of its online community. Most professional news outlets with pseudonymous commenting systems do not as a policy publicly divulge the real names of commenters who act unethically. Critics accused the *Tribune* of hypocrisy for arbitrarily outing a commenter to manufacture an attention-grabbing story while continuing to protect the identities of other commenters who spew hate-filled messages in the same forums. One critical comment on Facebook read:

> We love the Tribune, of course, but we're not really loving its decision today to out an anonymous online commenter. Generally, news publications fight efforts to expose identities of pseudonymous contributors to their comments section, arguing the anonymity encourages a more robust discourse. Some even invoke shield-law-type arguments to avoid identifying anonymous commenters to outsiders such as libel plaintiffs. But here it's the Tribune itself finding and then revealing the identity of "WhiskeyPete." Yes, his true identity is noteworthy during an election season—the story would not have led the paper's local section if it were not. And we get the public-interest argument the Trib makes for exposing WhiskeyPete. We just believe it is outweighed by the value of a marketplace of ideas in the comments section that is more open and diverse (and, yes, sometimes nasty) thanks to anonymous speech. The newspaper implies a promise of anonymity to its

online commenters who do not use their real names, and it should keep that promise—just as it would to a source offering information only upon condition of anonymity.[93]

Tribune publisher Terry Orme defended his newsroom's decision, writing in a column that the *Tribune* made no guarantee of anonymity to online commenters. Orme wrote,

> Our policy clearly states that we might be in touch with commenters about the things they post online. We make contact when a poster too often violates our policies, for example, or when we think that person might have something to offer to our reporting. We have complied with subpoenas from law enforcement when a commenter has threatened violence against someone.[94]

Orme agreed, however, that some audience members may have wrongly assumed "an implied protection of commenters' identities in that we allow anonymity in the first place."

"We had to weigh that assumption of implied protection against the possibility that the spokesman—a public figure who often is the voice of the city—had engaged in unethical, perhaps illegal, campaigning," Orme explained. "The larger issue is one of maintaining the public's trust in municipal employees and, in particular, those who work closely with an elected official."

When WhiskeyPete's unmasking occurred in July 2015, no specific language in the *Tribune*'s online commenting policy indicated users would lose anonymity if found in violation of commenting standards.[95] The standard penalty for bad behavior in most news site comment sections is not real-name accountability in a front-page news story; it's banning. Bad actors are kicked out of conversations. User submissions are deleted if flagged and found in violation of a site's terms of service. Repeat offenders are blocked from participating altogether. "*The Salt Lake Tribune* reserves the right to block a user from commenting if the staff believes the commenter is trying to disrupt the conversation with their behavior. . . . The *Tribune* may ban users at its discretion," stated the *Tribune's* Terms of Service.[96]

News sites, in general, offer privacy protections for anyone submitting an email address or other personal information in return for site access. Ethical and legal questions about anonymous comments tend to hinge on the explicit language of a news site's terms of service. The *Tribune* permitted commenters like Raymond to use pseudonyms in forums since the newspaper began publishing on the internet in the late 1990s. Commenters on *sltrib.com* had to register through third-party site Disqus and provide an email address for verification, but no real names were linked to the comments displayed to readers. The *Tribune*'s terms of service on comments did not guarantee commenters' anonymity either. It stated: "Your email address may be used to contact you regarding your registration or in regards to comments you have posted on our message boards or comments."

A situation similar to the *Tribune*'s WhiskeyPete drama happened eight years earlier at the *Post and Courier* in Charleston, South Carolina. Editors at the *Post and Courier* also chose to unmask a public employee who used the pseudonym afternoondelight to sound off on hundreds of online articles.[97] Frank O. Hunt was a press secretary who served as spokesperson for Charleston's top prosecutor. Most of Hunt's afternoondelight submissions appeared on stories about crime and pending court cases, including legal cases directly tied to his office. His comments were sometimes tinged with racism and sexism. The worst of Hunt's anonymous missives attacked the credibility of a sexual assault victim.

When the newsroom learned of Hunt's anonymous comments from a tipster, reporters easily linked Hunt's comment registration email address to his pseudonym and his anonymous commentary. After Hunt was outed in a news story, he told a competing news outlet that he was stunned the *Post and Courier* would reveal his online identity since he posted his comments with the expectation of confidentiality. "I will never post another one, I will tell you that," Hunt declared.[98]

The *Post and Courier*'s executive editor Bill Hawkins defended his newspaper's decision to reveal Hunt's online alias, saying the news organization would never go after a private citizen for similar anonymous comments. As a public official "abusing that position," Hunt presented a unique situation, Hawkins told the *Charleston City Paper*.[99] Public figures are considered fair game for journalistic inquiry and exposition. "Someone who holds a position of public trust would be better off writing a signed letter to the editor," Hawkins said.

Hunt also should have read the *Post and Courier*'s commenting terms of service more carefully. The news organization specifically states in its online policies that comments concerning stories "will not be considered confidential." A few weeks after the *Post and Courier* unmasked Hunt, he resigned from the position he had held for six years.[100]

A third example that served as a warning to digital news publishers happened in 2010 when *The Plain Dealer*, its website *Cleveland.com*, its editor-in-chief Susan Goldberg and its parent company Advance Publications found themselves at the receiving end of a $50 million lawsuit due to the unmasking of an anonymous commenter.[101] Reporters at the Ohio news organization had linked the IP and personal email address of Superior Court Judge Shirley Strickland Saffold to anonymous online comments posted on *Cleveland.com*.

Controversial online comments appeared on 80 stories under the pseudonym lawmiss, "and many involved Saffold's judicial rulings."[102] After a news story about the comments was published March 26, 2010, the judge denied having anything to do with them, saying her daughter was the source of the postings. In her lawsuit, Saffold argued *The Plain Dealer* had violated its own privacy policy by revealing to reporters that someone using her office computer and family email address was posting the comments. *The Plain Dealer* settled the lawsuit a year later for undisclosed terms. A donation was made to the Olivet Institutional Baptist Church choir in Saffold's name.[103]

News organizations do not have time or resources to unmask every anonymous commenter who violates their terms of service. But what transpired at the *Tribune* and in these other newsrooms raises ethical questions. If unacceptable and unethical behavior in online news discussion forums is worthy of drawing greater public attention in a news story, then enforcing rules equally should be the aspiration.

Perhaps bad behavior in anonymous news site comment sections could be contained if language about an "unmasking penalty" for rule breakers was clearly added to participation rules. Or maybe no one would comment at all.

Most news organizations only release the identifying information of a commenter if forced to do so by a court-ordered subpoena stemming from criminal or civil litigation. But not always. In September 2009, the *Wausau Daily Herald* in Wisconsin faced public backlash after the news outlet willingly handed over the email address of an anonymous online commenter. Here's how it happened. After the *Daily Herald* published a story about local politician Dean Zuleger, its website was flooded with anonymous comments viciously criticizing Zuleger. Outraged by the comments, Zuleger demanded to know the names of his critics. Editors supplied one critic's email address. Zuleger then sent the unmasked commenter—businessman Paul Klocko—a letter demanding he stop the personal attacks, "come out from behind the cloak" and meet him.[104] Klocko, of course, was shocked the *Daily Herald* had revealed his identity. The newspaper later apologized to Klocko for turning over his email address, and the *Daily Herald's* corporate parent, Gannett Company, clarified its policies on anonymous speech, saying its newsrooms would only release information if ordered by a court or if a comment contained a threat of imminent harm.[105]

Yet other news organizations have fought court orders to expose the real names of anonymous online commenters by utilizing "shield laws" to protect the identities of contributors. A shield law provides statutory protection for the "reporter's privilege"—legal rules that protect journalists against the government requiring them to reveal confidential sources or other information. According to the Society of Professional Journalists, "a shield law allows sources to feel safe approaching journalists to expose wrongdoing in society, similar to providing priests and psychiatrists the ability to provide some confidentiality to conversations."[106] Attorneys for Michael Mead, who was facing a North Carolina death penalty trial in a 2008 killing, had sought to force *The Gaston Gazette* to supply information that would expose the identity of an anonymous commenter on the *Gazette*'s website.[107] North Carolina Superior Court Judge Calvin Murphy ruled against the request after agreeing with the news organization's arguments that anonymous online comments on news sites are protected by the First Amendment and the state's journalism shield laws.[108]

Reporting information "on the condition of anonymity" may be an accepted tool journalists exercise in difficult and sensitive story situations, but there is clearly no industry-wide agreement on anonymous online comments on news stories. Investigative reporters go to great lengths to protect their anonymous news sources. Sometimes, news outlets will fight to protect their anonymous commenters. At other times, news sites will unmask anonymous transgressors deemed "newsworthy" or are forced to reveal commenter identities through discovery subpoenas. News organizations that have eliminated anonymous online comments avoid all the aforementioned drama and inconsistency, but those outlets are probably missing out on some authentic community conversation.

A bigger issue may be brought to bear if online publishers don't figure out their own ways to remedy the worst problems of anonymous online speech: a solution may be legislated for them.

"Governments, in particular, absolutely loathe the idea that people can speak without being identified. I fear there will soon be widespread laws disallowing anonymous speech even in America," media critic Dan Gillmor wrote in *The Guardian*.[109] Legislation to restrict online anonymity has already been floated. Two New York State legislators in May 2012 proposed a bill called the Internet Protection Act intended to force online publishers to unmask the authors of disparaging anonymous posts and remove posts from the web.[110] The legislators, in an attempt to throw a spotlight on "inappropriate and unjustified" uses of online anonymity, argued that anonymous internet speech mechanisms were being used to intimidate and harm New York citizens and businesses and that their legislation would provide a remedy to those who are unfairly and often harmfully attacked anonymously on the internet. Critics of the bill argued that in addition to violating the Constitutional right to free speech, the proposal would conveniently protect politicians from public criticism. The legislation failed, but it signaled that the tide may be turning away from complete immunity for online publishers.

In Search of Credibility

> We've hit a crossroads from celebrating the internet as the great equalizer that will give voice to everyone, to wondering if everyone needs a voice all of the time.
>
> —Annemarie Dooling, online communities expert[111]

Anonymous online comments are often audacious, as in "having a confident and daring quality that is often seen as shocking or rude."[112] The technology news site *Techdirt* deals with the audacity in an amusing way by allowing any visitor to post a comment without registering, but those who don't register will see their comment appear under the mocking heading "Anonymous Coward."

Among news sites that continue to host user comment forums, many have attempted to civilize the discourse by getting participants to give up some or all of their anonymity. With hopes that people will be deterred from polluting discussions if they can't be anonymous, news sites have layered more personal responsibility on commenters through real-name policies and social media authentication.

"The media industry as a whole is realizing that free speech without accountability is anything but free. The cost is a lack of civility and respect toward members of our community. That price is too high, and we are not alone in that feeling," noted the editors of the *Juneau Empire*, Alaska's capital city newspaper, when they ended anonymous comments and added a new policy restricting commenting to subscribers only. "Some will likely see this as an obstruction to free speech, though it is anything but. Individuals can still speak their mind within the boundary of our online commenting policy. The difference is the level of accountability for what is said."[113]

But as news organizations have forced people to register, use real names or log in using a Facebook account, it hasn't cured the cancer of incivility in most digital discussions. Norms are shifting. American news audiences may be past the stage of consequence-driven restraint in online discourse. Researchers have determined that Facebook comments—most of which reveal people's actual names, as well as their photos, workplace and familial connections—are actually nastier and meaner than the pseudonym-powered comments on most news websites.[114]

"There is a subset of people who are proud to be haters and who see real name attribution as a publicity opportunity," observed internet and privacy law expert Christopher Wolf.[115]

Does the credibility of a comment at the bottom of a news story depend on whether it is signed? I'm not convinced. The average citizen commenter won't be known to the mass audience anyway, so their "credibility" doesn't come from their name. Like contestants on NBC's *The Voice* or callers on talk radio, we don't need to know commenters' names, hometowns or what they look like to judge whether the ideas they post are worthwhile. In text-based environments, we judge commenters' credibility after reading what they have to say. Is the comment smart? Emotional? Snarky? Provocative? Condescending? Vulgar? Is it filled with typos and grammatical errors? Does it challenge our perspective or present some new information? Is it hateful? Although a person's identity in the offline world may ultimately shape their power in cyberspace, the combination of communication skills, persistence, idea quality and technical know-how can also determine influence in the digital space.

If the comment is signed by a well-known person—a celebrity or public figure—the audience is likely to prejudge the comment based on that person's existing reputation. If an ordinary citizen's title or location information is posted with the comment, that person's professional expertise or where they are from may influence their credibility. Silly or offensive avatars and pseudonyms can affect credibility, too. People who have credentials and expertise are only more credible if the audience is aware of their credentials.

Many small local news sites use Facebook's free commenting system. The Facebook commenting interface attempts to replicate real-world social norms by emphasizing some of the human qualities of conversation. People's faces, names and brief biographies are placed next to their public comments, establishing a baseline of responsibility. Facebook doesn't like anonymity because as an online social network, its purpose is to connect people. Anonymity is inherently antisocial, noted Miranda Katz.[116]

Facebook commenting threads can show a user's self-disclosed location and/or job title, which supplies the audience with useful credibility signals. But it is not uncommon for that self-disclosed information to be used by dissenting commenters with opposing agendas as ammunition to attack. I once saw a self-described clergyman post a hateful comment on a *USA Today* politics story and then get pummeled with insults from the crowd pointing out his hypocrisy.

Real-name policies on online forums, however, do make the threat of real-life offline consequences more of a possibility and may therefore constrain some online commenters from releasing a tirade or encourage others to be more thoughtful before posting. Facebook also encourages users to share their comments with friends. Users can opt out, but knowledge that comments could be broadcast to your larger network can be a deterrent to bad behavior.[117] If site hosts force online commenters to attach their real names and their professional or community reputations to comments in the public sphere, online commenters must take greater ownership of their opinions and any fallout as a result of broadcasting their ideas. Real-name ownership adds a level of societal consequences, whereas unsigned comments are essentially consequence free. When consequence-free speech becomes harassing, threatening or misleading, then it becomes harmful and not worthy of inclusion in a professional news product.

Media technology reporter Mathew Ingram has argued that by requiring real names, sites may decrease the potential for bad behavior, but they also significantly decrease the likelihood that many of their readers will comment. "Some may see this as a benefit—fewer comments to moderate—but it is also a risk, especially when engagement with a community of readers could mean the difference between life and death for a media outlet," Ingram observed.

In July 2013, after I reported on *ESPN*'s switch to a Facebook-authentication commenting system,[118] I received emotional feedback from disappointed *ESPN* commenters who said the network was ruining their online community experience. "*ESPN* will lose all my traffic with this move. I've met people over the 7–8 years I've been there that I'll never be able to speak to again. I refuse to restart a Facebook account just to use *ESPN* comments. I just won't go to *ESPN* anymore if this goes through," wrote one commenter.[119]

Another wrote to me in an email, "Unfortunately, this *was* a fun place to banter with other teams' fans. . . . I understand that websites may prefer wringing their hands of the whole issue by switching to Facebook, but all they are doing is upsetting the customers, the good guys. The bad guys can still post with fake accounts. Currently, there is no more sharing of ideas on *ESPN.com*, and the comments/traffic has shifted to *CNNSI.com*. They will all move again if *Sports Illustrated* follows *ESPN*'s lead. . . . My conclusion? This is political correctness run amok."

Can you be anonymous online and act with responsibility? Of course. But do journalists and audiences even agree on a coherent theory of digital responsibility? Digital citizenship is a topic online news organizations should be discussing with their readers, viewers, fans and critics.

It is hard to sustain a network and build relationships while engaging in discourse without a name. Smaller anonymous or pseudonymous groups that form around a specific interest tend to fare better than in the open market of conversation, where a person's identity matters less than their willingness to engage about a shared passion. Some of the most civil anonymous discussions I've encountered online (which include plenty of disagreement) are the fans of TV shows who respectfully discuss the latest episode below recaps posted by news sites.

In my view, the importance of anonymity for commenters depends upon the nature and character of the site and the topics discussed. If the site is hosting a volatile political discussion and sharing an opinion or observation that would put a commenter's life or livelihood in danger, then that's a worthy reason to grant anonymity to a commenter. A news site can permit anonymity if it premoderates all the comments coming in, like screening callers in talk radio.[120] Journalists generally don't grant sources anonymity without first finding out their motive for wanting to remain secret.

Legal scholar Danielle Keats Citron has suggested online intermediaries adopt anonymity as their default setting for contributions but make it an explicit privilege that can be lost if a user's anonymous speech harms others in ways the news site finds unacceptable. By adding a clear penalty, such a policy could preserve the upside potential of anonymity and obstruct its downside.[121]

Another possibility is to offer the public two different sets of online commentary—one anonymous, the other with identifiability. Gawker Media's Kinja system provides a version of this idea, with one set of comments moderated by the author of the article and a separate stream of unmoderated comments. Depending on the sensibilities of the audience, readers can choose between seeing real-name comments or anonymous ones. Or a comment system can be designed to give priority to real-name commenters and push anonymous contributions to the bottom of the comment stream. This preserves users' ability to comment anonymously but adds the consequence of obscurity.

Most professional news organizations want to create online spaces where communities of people will thoughtfully engage with each other. Not all contributors are wise. Not all contributors are considerate. Not all posts contain useful information. Not all conversations are civilized debates. If a news site can't commit to consistent moderation, then it should not offer anonymity to contributors. The research on anonymity shows we cannot depend on the honor system. If news purveyors don't consistently apply standards or pay attention to their own digital discussions, the vicious and vulgar voices will rule. "The more you consider comments part of your news product, the more the comments section should reflect your journalistic ethics,"[122] professor Paula Poindexter advised in the Online News Association's "Build Your Own Ethics Code."

In 2013, the trend among news organizations was to rid themselves of anonymous commenters. Since 2014, the trend has shifted to eliminating on-site public discourse areas entirely. In the end, it's up to individual digital news publishers to make the call on the value of anonymity in both news reports and online comment sections. The internet's fickle attention economy will judge whether the choice was the right one.

Notes

1. Wells, H. G. "Chapter 21." *The Invisible Man: A Grotesque Romance*. Lit2Go Edition. 1897. Web. http://etc.usf.edu/lit2go/120/the-invisible-man/2501/chapter-21

2. *Sltrib.com* comment policy states: "Reader comments on sltrib.com are the opinions of the writer, not The Salt Lake Tribune. We will delete comments containing obscenities, personal attacks and inappropriate or offensive remarks. Flagrant or repeat violators will be banned." It also states, "The Salt Lake Tribune does not screen comments before they are posted. You are more likely to see inappropriate comments before our staff does, so we ask that you click the arrow in the top right corner of a comment to submit those comments for moderator review."

3. Archive of Disqus comments by WhiskeyPete. Web. https://disqus.com/by/WhiskeyPete/

4. Smith, Sydney. "Salt Lake Tribune Outs Anonymous Commenter as Mayor's Spokesperson Art Raymond." *IMediaEthics*. 1 Aug. 2015. Web. www.imedia ethics.org/salt-lake-tribune-outs-anonymous-commenter-as-mayors-spokes-person-art-raymond/

5. Schott, Bryan. "Editor's Column: 'WhiskeyPete' Was Always Hiding in Plain Sight." *Utahpolicy.com*. 3 Aug. 2015. Web. http://utahpolicy.com/index.php/features/today-at-utah-policy/6545-editor-s-column-whiskeypete-was-always-hiding-in-plain-sight

6. "Online Comments By 'WhiskeyPete' Aka Art Raymond." Uploaded to Scribd Account of *The Salt Lake Tribune*. 31 Jul. 2015. Web. www.scribd.com/document/273098860/Online-comments-by-WhiskeyPete-aka-Art-Raymond

7. McKellar, Katie. "Salt Lake City Mayor's Spokesman Placed on Administrative Leave after Online Comments." *Deseret News*. 31 Jul. 2015. Web. www.deseretnews.com/article/865633628/Salt-Lake-City-mayors-spokesman-placed-on-administrative-leave-after-online-comments.html?pg=all

8. Semerad, Tony. "Flagged Online Post Revealed Mayoral Spokesman's Anonymous Campaign Sniping." *The Salt Lake Tribune*. 30 Jul. 2015. Web. www.sltrib.com/home/2787085-155/flagged-online-post-revealed-mayoral-spokesmans
   Also, Carlisle, Nate. "Salt Lake City Spokesman Placed on Leave during Probe of Anonymous Online Political Comments." *The Salt Lake Tribune*. 30 Jul. 2015. Web. www.sltrib.com/home/2786327-155/salt-lake-city-spokesman-placed-on

9. Raymond was placed on paid administrative leave after the story was published while the city launched an investigation of whether he used "public resources for electioneering." He was later demoted. See Ibid.

10. Pfitzmann, Andreas, and Marit Köhntopp. "Anonymity, Unobservability, and Pseudonymity: A Proposal for Terminology." *Designing Privacy Enhancing Technologies*. Volume 2009 of the series Lecture Notes in Computer Science. 16 Mar. 2001. 1–9. Web. http://link.springer.com/chapter/10.1007%2F3-540-44702-4_1

11. Qian, Hua, and Craig R. Scott. "Anonymity and Self-Disclosure on Weblogs." *Journal of Computer Mediated Communication*. Jul. 2007. Volume 12, Issue 4. Web. http://onlinelibrary.wiley.com/doi/10.1111/j.1083-6101.2007.00380.x/full

12. Lapidot-Lefler, Noam, and Azy Barak. "Effects of Anonymity, Invisibility, and Lack of Eye-Contact on Toxic Online Disinhibition." *Computers in Human Behavior*. Mar. 2012. Volume 28, Issue 2. Web. www.sciencedirect.com/science/article/pii/S0747563211002317

13. Pitts, Leonard, Jr. "Den of Anonymity." *Pittsburgh Post-Gazette*. 2 Apr. 2010. Web. www.post-gazette.com/opinion/Op-Ed/2010/04/02/Leonard-Pitts-Jr-Den-of-anonymity/stories/201004020121

14. Goldberg, Stephanie. "News Sites Reining in Nasty User Comments." *CNN*. 19 Jul. 2010. Web. www.cnn.com/2010/TECH/web/07/19/commenting.on. news.sites/index.html
15. Harrop, Froma. "Web Anonymity: The Devil Made Me Post It." *The Seattle Times*. 12 Mar. 2012. Web. http://old.seattletimes.com/html/opinion/20177340 48_harrop13.html
16. Heatherly, Kyle A., Anthony L. Fargo, and Jason A. Martin. "Anonymous Online Comments: The Law and Best Media Practices from Around the World." *International Press Institute*. Oct. 2014. Web. http://ipi.freemedia.at/ fileadmin/user_upload/IPI_AnonymousSpeech_Oct2014.pdf
17. "Watergate at 40." *The Washington Post*. 12 Jun. 2012. Web. www.washington post.com/politics/watergate/
18. Daniel Okrent. "Weapons of Mass Destruction? Or Mass Distraction?" *New York Times*. 30 May 2004. Web. www.nytimes.com/2004/05/30/weekinreview/ the-public-editor-weapons-of-mass-destruction-or-mass-distraction.html
19. Carlson, Matt. "The Problems—and Promise—of Unnamed Sources." *On the Condition of Anonymity: Unnamed Sources and the Battle for Journalism*. Champaign: University of Illinois Press, 2012. 1–30. Print.
20. Ibid.
21. Ibid.
22. Ibid.
23. "Gamesmanship-Definition." *Merriam Webster Dictionary*. Web. www. merriam-webster.com/dictionary/gamesmanship
24. Carlson. "The Problems—and Promise—of Unnamed Sources."
25. Sullivan, Margaret. "Tightening the Screws on Anonymous Sources." *The New York Times*. 15 Mar. 2016. Web. http://publiceditor.blogs.nytimes.com/ 2016/03/15/new-york-times-anoymous-sources-policy-public-editor/
26. Carlson. "The Problems—and Promise—of Unnamed Sources."
27. Farrell, Michael. "Anonymous Sources." SPJ Ethics Committee Position Papers. *Society of Professional Journalists*. 10 May 2013. Web. www.spj.org/ethics-papers-anonymity.asp
28. Carlson. "The Problems—and Promise—of Unnamed Sources."
29. Buckels, Erin E., Paul D. Trapnell, and Delroy L. Paulhus. "Trolls Just Want to Have Fun." *Personality and Individual Differences*. Sept. 2014, Volume 67. Web. https://doi.org/10.1016/j.paid.2014.01.016
30. Heatherly, Fargo, and Martin. "Anonymous Online Comments."
31. Santana, Arthur D. "Virtuous or Vitriolic." *Journalism Practice*. 18 Jul. 2013. Volume 8, Issue 1. Web. www.tandfonline.com/doi/abs/10.1080/17512786.20 13.813194
32. Sounding Board Survey on Online Comments. Associated Press Media Editors. 17 Jul. 2014. Web. www.apme.com/?page=update071714
33. Reader, Bill. "Gatekeeping in an Age without Fences." *Audience Feedback in the News Media*. New York: Routledge, Taylor & Francis Group, 2015. 168–77. Print.
34. Heatherly, Fargo, and Martin. "Anonymous Online Comments."
35. Poniewozik, James. "Halt and Catch Fire Became the Next Mad Men When It Stopped Trying to Be." *Time*. 3 Aug. 2015. Web. http://time.com/3980486/ review-halt-and-catch-fire-season-2-finale
36. Erard, Michael. "No Comments." *New York Times*. 20 Sept. 2013. Web. www. nytimes.com/2013/09/22/magazine/no-comments.html?pagewanted=all&_r=0

37. Rainie, Lee, Sara Kiesler, Ruogu Kang, and Mary Madden. "The Quest for Anonymity Online." *Pew Research Center*. 5 Sept. 2013. Web. www.pewinternet. org/2013/09/05/part-1-the-quest-for-anonymity-online/

38. Drake, Bruce. "What Strategies Do YOU Use to Protect Your Online Identity?" *Pew Research Center*. Center. 5 Sept. 2013. Web. www.pewresearch. org/fact-tank/2013/09/05/what-strategies-do-you-use-to-protect-your-online-identity/

39. Wormald, Benjamin. "Attempts to Obscure Data Collection and Preserve Anonymity." *Pew Research Center*. 20 May 2015. Web. www.pewinternet. org/2015/05/20/attempts-to-obscure-data-collection-and-preserve-anonymity

40. Ingram, Mathew. "Research Shows That If You Remove Anonymity You Won't Hear from Most of Your Readers." *Gigaom*. 27 Aug. 2014. Web. https:// gigaom.com/2014/08/27/research-shows-that-if-you-remove-anonymity-you-wont-hear-from-most-of-your-readers/

41. Shanahan, Marie K. "More News Organizations Try Civilizing Online Comments with the Help of Social Media." *The Poynter Institute*. 16 Jul. 2013. Web. www.poynter.org/2013/more-news-organizations-try-civilizing-online-comments-with-the-help-of-social-media/218284/

42. Fishkin, James S. *When the People Speak: Deliberative Democracy and Public Consultation*. Oxford; New York: Oxford University Press, 2009. 18. Print.

43. Ibid.

44. Hampton, Keith, Lee Rainie, Weixue Lu, Maria Dwyer, Inyoung Shin, and Kristen Purcell. "Main Analysis: Political Issues and the Spiral of Silence." *Pew Research Center*. 26 Aug. 2014. Web. www.pewinternet.org/2014/08/26/main-analysis-political-issues-and-the-spiral-of-silence/

45. Miller, Jason C. "Who's Exposing John Doe? Distinguishing Between Public and Private Figure Plaintiffs in Subpoenas to ISPs in Anonymous Online Defamation Suits." *Journal of Technology Law & Policy*. 9 Dec. 2008. Volume 13, Issue 1. Web. http://ssrn.com/abstract=1365326

46. Ibid.

47. Pierson, Emma. "Outnumbered but Well-Spoken: Female Commenters in the New York Times." In *Proceedings of the 18th ACM Conference on Computer Supported Cooperative Work & Social Computing (CSCW '15)*. ACM, New York, NY. 2015. Web. http://cs.stanford.edu/people/emmap1/cscw_paper.pdf

48. Reich, Zvi. "User Comments: The Transformation of Participatory Space." In Jane B. Singer, Alfred Hermida, David Domingo, Ari Heinonen, Steve Paulussen, Thorsten Quandt, Zvi Reich, and Marina Vujnovic (Eds.), *Participatory Journalism: Guarding Open Gates at Online Newspapers*. Malden, MA: Wiley-Blackwell, 2011. Web. http://dx.doi.org/10.1002/9781444340747.ch6

49. Reader, Bill. "Free Press vs. Free Speech? The Rhetoric of 'Civility' in Regard to Anonymous Online Comments." *Journalism & Mass Communication Quarterly*. 22 May 2012. Volume 89, Issue 3. Web. http://journals.sagepub. com/doi/abs/10.1177/1077699012447923

50. Matias, J. Nathan. "The Real Name Fallacy." *The Coral Project*. 3 Jan. 2017. Web. https://blog.coralproject.net/the-real-name-fallacy/

51. Policinski, Gene. "Drawing the 'Online' Line on Free Speech." *First Amendment Center*. 10 Jan. 2010. Web. www.firstamendmentcenter.org/drawing-the-%E2%80%98online%E2%80%99-line-on-free-speech/

52. Worcester, Wayne. Email exchanges and conversations, Mar. 2012.

53. Ibid.

54. Coscarelli, Joe. "Eminem Collaborates on the Album for the Film 'Southpaw'." *New York Times*. 18 Jul. 2015. Web. www.nytimes.com/2015/07/19/arts/music/eminem-collaborates-on-the-album-for-the-film-southpaw.html

55. Newton, Eric. "Let's Get It Right with Real Names." *Knight Foundation*. 28 Oct. 2011. Web. www.knightfoundation.org/articles/lets-get-it-right-real-names-2012

56. Ibid.

57. SPJ Code of Ethics. Society of Professional Journalists. 6 Sept. 2014. Web. www.spj.org/ethicscode.asp

58. Newton. "Let's Get It Right with Real Names."

59. Heatherly, Fargo, and Martin. "Anonymous Online Comments."

60. Christie, John. "Anonymous Sources: Leaving Journalism's False God Behind." *The Poynter Institute*. 23 Apr. 2014. Web. www.poynter.org/2014/anonymous-sources-leaving-journalisms-false-god-behind/249037/

61. Suler, John. "The Online Disinhibition Effect." *CyberPsychology & Behavior*. Jun. 2004. Volume 7, Issue 3. 321–6. Web. https://doi.org/10.1089/1094931041291295

62. Carlson. "The Problems—and Promise—of Unnamed Sources."

63. Chen, Adrian. "Meet the Dogged Researchers Who Try to Unmask Haters Online." *MIT Technology Review*. 3 Nov. 2016. Web. www.technologyreview.com/s/533426/the-troll-hunters/

64. Santana. "Virtuous or Vitriolic."

65. Lapidot-Lefler, and Barak. "Effects of Anonymity, Invisibility, and Lack of Eye-Contact on Toxic Online Disinhibition."

66. Krahulik, Mike, and Jerry Holkins. "John Gabriel's Greater Internet Fuckwad Theory." *Penny Arcade*. Mar. 2004. Web. www.penny-arcade.com/comic/2004/03/19

67. Plato. "The Republic, Book II." *The Internet Classics Archive*. Translated by Benjamin Jowett. Daniel C. Stevenson. Web. http://classics.mit.edu/Plato/republic.3.ii.html

68. Ibid.

69. Lee, Eun-Ju. "That's Not the Way It Is: How User-Generated Comments on the News Affect Perceived Media Bias." *Journal of Computer Mediated Communication*. 10 Oct. 2012. Volume 18. Web. http://onlinelibrary.wiley.com/doi/10.1111/j.1083-6101.2012.01597.x/abstract

70. Anderson, Ashley A., Dominique Brossard, Dietram A. Scheufele, Michael A. Xenos, and Peter Ladwig. "The 'Nasty Effect': Online Incivility and Risk Perceptions of Emerging Technologies." *Journal of Computer Mediated Communication*. Apr. 2014. Volume 19, Issue 3. Web. http://onlinelibrary.wiley.com/doi/10.1111/jcc4.12009/abstract

71. Wallsten, Kevin, and Melinda Tarsi. "Persuasion from Below." *Journalism Practice*. 6 Nov. 2015, Volume 10, Issue 8. Web. www.tandfonline.com/doi/abs/10.1080/17512786.2015.1102607?journalCode=rjop20

    Also, Wallsten, Kevin, and Melinda Tarsi. "It's Time to End Anonymous Comments Sections." *The Washington Post*. 19 Aug. 2014. Web. www.washingtonpost.com/news/monkey-cage/wp/2014/08/19/its-time-to-end-anonymous-comments-sections/

72. Christie, John. "Anonymous Sources: Leaving Journalism's False God Behind."

73. Anderson, Brossard, Scheufele, Xenos, and Ladwig. "The Nasty Effect."

74. Haines, Russell, Jill Hough, Lan Cao, and Douglas Haines. "Anonymity in Computer-Mediated Communication: More Contrarian Ideas with Less Influence."

Group Decision and Negotiation. Jul. 2014, Volume 23, Issue 4. Web. http://dx.doi.org/10.1007/s10726-012-9318-2

75. Ibid.
76. Cavna, Michael. "'Nobody Knows You're a Dog': At 20, Web Cartoon as True as Ever." *The Washington Post*. WP Company, 31 Jul. 2013. Web. www.washingtonpost.com/blogs/comic-riffs/post/nobody-knows-youre-a-dog-as-iconic-internet-cartoon-turns-20-creator-peter-steiner-knows-the-joke-rings-as-relevant-as-ever/2013/07/31/73372600-f98d-11e2-8e84-c56731a202fb_blog.html
    Also, Steiner, Peter. "On the Internet, Nobody Knows You're a Dog." *The New Yorker*. 5 Jul. 1993. Web. http://archives.newyorker.com/?iid=15713&st artpage=page0000063
77. *McIntyre v. Ohio Elections Commission, 514 U.S. 334 (1995)*. Full text of decision available at www.law.cornell.edu/supct/html/93-986.ZO.html
78. Chen, Adrian. "Unmasking Reddit's Violentacrez, the Biggest Troll on the Web." *Gawker*. 12 Oct. 2012. Web. http://gawker.com/5950981/unmasking-reddits-violentacrez-the-biggest-troll-on-the-web
79. Swash, Rosie. "A New Internet Age? Web Users Turn on 'Trolls'." *The Guardian*. 19 Oct. 2012. Web. www.theguardian.com/technology/2012/oct/19/new-internet-age-trolls
80. Holpuch, Amanda. "Reddit User Violentacrez Fired from Job after Gawker Exposé." *The Guardian*. 16 Oct. 2012. Web. www.theguardian.com/technology/2012/oct/16/reddit-violentacrez-gawker-expose
81. Statt, Nick. "Reddit Bans Two Prominent Alt-Right Subreddits." *The Verge*. Vox Media. 1 Feb. 2017. Web. www.theverge.com/2017/2/1/14478948/reddit-alt-right-ban-altright-alternative-right-subreddits-doxing
82. "47 U.S. Code § 230: Protection for Private Blocking and Screening of Offensive Material." *Legal Information Institute*. Cornell Law School. Web. www.law.cornell.edu/uscode/text/47/230
83. Ibid.
84. Kim, Nancy S. "Imposing Tort Liability on Websites for Cyberharassment." *Yale Law Journal*. 17 Nov. 2009. Pocket Part, Volume 118, 115. Web. http://ssrn.com/abstract=1507463
85. Hilden, Julie. "Why You Can't Sue Google: The Reason Defamation Law Applies to News Sites, But Not News Search Sites, and What This May Mean for the Future." *FindLaw.com*. 25 May 2004. Web. http://writ.news.findlaw.com/hilden/20040525.html
86. "Bloggers Legal Guide: Online Defamation Law." *Electronic Frontier Foundation*. 12 Jun. 2005. Web. www.eff.org/issues/bloggers/legal/liability/defamation
87. King, Ryan W. "Online Defamation: Bringing the Communications Decency Act of 1996 In Line with Sound Public Policy." *Duke University Law & Technology Review*. Oct. 2003. Web. www.law.duke.edu/journals/dltr/articles/2003dltr0024.html
88. Davis, Wendy. "Anonymous Commenting Under Scrutiny by Illinois Court." *MediaPost*. 26 Mar. 2009. Web. www.mediapost.com/publications/?fa=Articles.showArticle&art_aid=102879
89. Maxon v. Ottawa Publishing Company. 2008. Case description and court documents posted by *Citizen Media Law Project*. Web. www.citmedialaw.org/threats/maxon-v-ottawa-publishing-company
90. "Court Ignores Trend on Anonymous Comments." *Reporters Committee for Freedom of the Press*. 10 Jun. 2010. Web. www.rcfp.org/newsitems/index.php?i=11446

91. Ibid.
92. "In Defamation Case, Anonymous Comments Not OK: Appellate Court Rules Newspaper Must Disclose Names." *Chicago Tribune*. 2 Jun. 2010. Web. http://articles.chicagotribune.com/2010-06-02/news/ct-met-ottawa-anonymous-comment-0603-20100602_1_defamation-case-court-appellate
93. Facebook post by "Save the Salt Lake Tribune." 31 Jul. 2015. Web. www.facebook.com/savethesaltlaketribune/posts/1054834097870333
94. Orme, Terry. "Editor column: Decision to reveal commenter's identity not made lightly." *Salt Lake Tribune*. 1 Aug. 2015. Web. http://archive.sltrib.com/article.php?id=2790186&itype=CMSID
95. "About Comments." *Salt Lake Tribune* terms of service. Web. www.sltrib.com/info/aboutcomments/
96. Ibid.
97. Smith, Glenn. "Online Comments No 'Delight'." *The Post & Courier*. 3 Dec. 2007. Web. www.postandcourier.com/article/20071204/PC1602/312049994
98. Haire, Chris. "P&C Reveals Internet Poster." *Charleston City Paper*. 12 Dec. 2007. Web. www.charlestoncitypaper.com/charleston/pc-reveals-internet-poster/Content?oid=1112428
99. Ibid.
100. "Briefly: Solicitor's Office Press Officer Resigns." *The Post & Courier*. 18 Dec. 2007. Web. www.postandcourier.com/article/20071219/PC1602/312199977
101. Davis, Wendy. "Judge Sues Cleveland Plain Dealer for Unmasking Her." *MediaPost*. 8 Apr. 2010. Web. www.mediapost.com/publications/?fa=Articles.showArticle&art_aid=125773
102. McCarthy, James F. "Anonymous Online Comments Are Linked to the Personal Email Account of Cuyahoga County Common Pleas Judge Shirley Strickland Saffold." *Plain Dealer*. 26 Mar. 2010. Web. http://blog.cleveland.com/metro/2010/03/post_258.html
103. Kiesow, Damon. "Plain Dealer Settles Comment Lawsuit, Limits of Anonymity Untested." The *Poynter Institute*. 3 Jan 2011. Web. www.poynter.org/2011/plain-dealer-settles-comment-lawsuit-limits-of-anonymity-untested/112641/
104. Foley, Ryan J. "Wisconsin Paper Faces Backlash for Outing 'Anonymous' Web Critic of Suburban Official." *Associated Press* via cleveland.com. 19 Sept. 2009. Web. www.cleveland.com/nation/index.ssf/2009/09/wisconsin_paper_faces_backlash.html
105. "Zuleger v. Klocko." *Digital Media Law Project*. 4 Dec. 2009. Web. www.dmlp.org/threats/zuleger-v-klocko#node_legal_threat_full_group_description
106. "Shield Law 101: Frequently Asked Questions." *Society of Professional Journalists*. 30 May 2013. Web. www.spj.org/shieldlaw-faq.asp
107. Ellis, Kevin. "Judge Gives Online Commenters First Amendment Protection." *First Amendment Coalition*. 29 Jul. 2010. Web. https://firstamendmentcoalition.org/2010/07/judge-gives-online-commenters-first-amendment-protection/
     Also, 'Gaston Gazette' Wins Ruling in Anonymous-Comments Case. Associated Press via *Editor & Publisher*. 2 Aug. 2010. Web. www.editorandpublisher.com/news/gaston-gazette-wins-ruling-in-anonymous-comments-case/
108. "Judge Gives Online Newspaper Opinion Posters Protection Under Constitution." *The Raleigh Telegram*. 2 Aug. 2010. Web. via archive.org. http://web.archive.org/web/20101218054030/www.raleightelegram.com/2010072908.html
109. Gillmor, Dan. "In Defence of Anonymity, Despite 'Gay Girl in Damascus'." *The Guardian*. 15 Jun. 2011. Web. www.theguardian.com/commentisfree/cifamerica/2011/jun/15/blogging-press-freedom-amina

110. New York Senate Bill S6779. 2011–2012 Legislative Session. Web. www.nysenate.gov/legislation/bills/2011/S6779.
    Also, Verrette, Amanda. "Bill Would Eliminate Derogatory, Anonymous Web Posts." *Legislative Gazette*. 14 May 2012. Web. via Archive.org. http://goo.gl/uLF2jr. Accessed 5/15/2012.
    Also, Gates, Sara. "Anonymous Comment Ban: Internet Protection Act Threatens Online Anonymity For New York-Based Websites." *The Huffington Post*. 24 May 2012. Web. www.huffingtonpost.com/2012/05/24/anonymous-comment-ban-legislation-new-york_n_1543033.html
    Also, Hartmann, Margaret. "New York Legislators Hope to End Internet Anonymity, Thwart Nasty Commenters." *New York Magazine*. 23 May 2012. Web. http://nymag.com/daily/intelligencer/2012/05/ny-bill-takes-aim-at-nasty-online-commenters.html

111. Dooling, Annemarie. "Don't Identify by Names Online but by Knowledge." *New York Times*. 19 Aug. 2014. Web. www.nytimes.com/roomfordebate/2014/08/19/the-war-against-online-trolls/dont-identify-by-names-online-but-by-knowledge

112. "Definition of Audacity." *Merriam Webster Dictionary*. Web. www.merriam-webster.com/dictionary/audacity

113. "Empire Editorial: Anonymous Commenting Ends Sunday." *Juneau Empire*. 29 Jan. 2014. Web. http://juneauempire.com/opinion/2014-01-29/empire-editorial-anonymous-commenting-ends-sunday

114. Rost, Katja, Lea Stahel, and Bruno S. Frey. "Digital Social Norm Enforcement: Online Firestorms in Social Media." *PLoS One*. Public Library of Science. 17 Jun. 2016. Web. http://dx.doi.org/10.1371/journal.pone.0155923.

115. Wolf, Christopher. "Anonymity May Have Killed Online Commenting." *New York Times*. 18 Apr. 2016. Web. www.nytimes.com/roomfordebate/2016/04/18/have-comment-sections-on-news-media-websites-failed/anonymity-may-have-killed-online-commenting

116. Katz, Miranda. "These Failed Apps Discovered a Hidden Rule of the Web." *Backchannel*. 10 Mar. 2017. Web. https://backchannel.com/these-failed-apps-discovered-a-hidden-rule-of-the-web-391471ca5952#.p2ayjnge0

117. Zhuo, Julie. "Where Anonymity Breeds Contempt." *New York Times*. 29 Nov. 2010. Web. www.nytimes.com/2010/11/30/opinion/30zhuo.html

118. Shanahan. "More News Organizations Try Civilizing Online Comments."

119. Forever, Mike. "ESPN and Facebook: Don't Convert the Comment Section into Facebook Comments Only for Private Reasons!" *Change.org Petition*. 3 Jul. 2013. Web. www.change.org/petitions/espn-and-facebook-don-t-convert-the-comment-section-into-facebook-comments-only-for-private-reasons

120. Shanahan, Marie K. "How Talk Radio Listens to Its Audience, Provides Lessons for Online Publishers." *The Poynter Institute*. 4 Mar. 2014. Web. www.poynter.org/2014/how-talk-radio-listens-to-its-audience-provides-lessons-for-online-publishers/241945/

121. Citron, Danielle Keats. "Sunday Dialogue: Anonymity and Incivility on the Internet." *New York Times*. 21 Nov. 2011. Web. www.nytimes.com/2011/11/27/opinion/sunday/sunday-dialogue-anonymity-and-incivility-on-the-internet.html

122. Poindexter, Paula. "Online Commenting." *Build Your Own Ethics Code Project*. Online News Association. 24 Sept. 2015. Web. http://ethics.journalists.org/topics/online-commenting/

6   Debugging Digital Discourse

> A bug is never just a mistake. It represents something bigger. . . . The bug forces the software to adapt, evolving something new because of it. Work around it or work through it. No matter what, it changes, it becomes something new, the next version, the inevitable upgrade.
> —Elliot Alderson (Rami Malek), *Mr. Robot*, Season 1, Episode 3[1]

Journalism's online comment conundrum is a many-headed hydra of problems in need of innovative solutions. To scale open public participation with civility and within an ethical journalistic framework, there are design flaws to debug, saboteurs to outsmart and a host of psychological and sociological forces to understand. Journalists face the complicated task of respecting free speech while at the same time filtering out abusive comments and misinformation. Comment streams can be commandeered by trolls, but they are also at the mercy of manipulative intellectuals and political charlatans who muffle information and impersonate the public will. There are members of the audience who have no interest in engaging in meaningful dialogue, while others scream "troll!" at anyone who disagrees with them.

There are legitimate reasons why so many news organizations have chosen to ditch comments on their sites and send conversations to social media platforms like Facebook and Twitter. Off-topic posts and toxic commentary undermine legitimate news reporting. Design flaws in commenting software enable too many bad actors. Strained newsrooms can't afford to devote limited human resources to policing comment sections. At war with incivility, the struggle to keep discussion areas useful is exhausting and demoralizing for journalists.

"History has shown that some of the biggest challenges to the First Amendment occur during times of technological change," noted Thomas C. Rubin, a steering committee member of the Reporters Committee for Freedom of the Press.[2] If news reports are an essential component of a vibrant public sphere, and if citizens of a democracy are obliged to comment on every matter within the public sphere, then news organizations in the digital age should be providing forums in which civil public discourse can take place. A traditional function of the press in society is to foster discussion and debate on issues of public concern.[3] One of journalism's core democratic responsibilities includes providing forums for public criticism and compromise.[4] That obligation hasn't disappeared in the digital age. It's become even more important.

Viral fake news outperformed real news stories on Facebook at the end of the 2016 U.S. presidential campaign.[5] That's a burning signal the marketplace of digital information and discourse is not working properly. Public digital discourse is an aspect of "audience engagement" in need of more nurturing by news organizations as the civic norms for our deliberative democracy erode. Our digitally connected citizenry is going to have a hard time solving problems if people are unable, unwilling or incapable of virtual online listening, talking and identifying where they actually agree. Those who wonder how anyone can take digital conversation seriously need look no farther than @realdonaldtrump's Twitter feed[6] to know public online dialogue exerts power and consequences in the offline world.

Can better news experiences be designed with conversation, feedback and deliberation as part of the equation? Most news organizations focus their attention on developing new ways to do the core acts of journalism—reporting, packaging and distributing stories. Public discourse needs greater attention as an innovation in digital news media, too. More opportunities for news-driven civic conversation can lead to increased public participation in democratic decisions. If citizens are actively engaged in a context in which they feel their voice matters, they may feel compelled to continue engagement and increase participation.[7]

Discovery, including reading and responding to online comments, is part of the modern news experience. Comments provide another reason to read/watch/listen to news as a resource of added value. Come for the story; stay for the discussion about it. Journalists working in the digital space, like their offline counterparts, have found success in building greater user loyalty and audience engagement through opinion, dialogue and "emotional involvement."[8] Online comments embody all three of these characteristics.

Citizens of a democracy should be exposed to a variety of viewpoints. It's important for unpopular ideas to get a hearing. "It's important for there to be debate, and changes of heart, and to allow sincere disagreements to continue to wrestle with one another for clarification," wrote graphic artist Tucker FitzGerald in a post on Medium.[9] It's also important for points of consensus to be highlighted, so we recognize where opposing camps can actually agree. The internet has within it the ability to counter people's propensity to avoid opposing ideas and difficult conversations. "Unanticipated encounters, involving topics and points of view we have not sought out and perhaps find irritating are central to democracy and even to freedom itself," argued political scholar Cass R. Sunstein.[10] News organizations in the digital space can fight echo chambers and pop filter bubbles through concerted efforts to expose audiences to diverse perspectives and by adding more voices to the public discourse.

Local news organizations especially are depended upon to build a sense of community among citizens. This can be accomplished in part by engaging people in a common online conversation. Journalists can moderate. While citizens' comments tend to be motivated by emotion, biases and—in the case of trolls—disruption, journalists, at their best, are trained in verification and reasoned debate and "possess an ethos of open-minded inquiry."[11] Trained journalists at the helm of a discussion can purposefully present various sides of an issue or topic. They can classify opinion, conjecture and hearsay. They can question and fact-check, label verified information and keep the record straight. The quality and depth of a debate improves with the knowledge and skill of its participants.

Breaking away from old conventions is hard, but news in 2017 does not need to follow the same production cycle of a decade ago. Journalists are operating in a hyperconnected world of ubiquitous media, global connectivity, virtual simulacra and instantaneous communication.[12] Technology is influencing everything, creating radical changes in the strictures dictating our lives. If a journalist is prompting a conversation by producing a story and promoting it on social media but not setting the tone for the discussion, the discourse isn't going to elevate itself. Journalist moderators who watch over comment submissions and guide conversations can act as teachers in classrooms, nudging participants to be civil and on point. "Journalism is moderated conversation," argued Marcy Burstiner, chair of the journalism department at Humboldt State University. "When you don't moderate, then it's just public discussion, and there are lots of forums for public discussion."[13]

The responsibility for productive audience interactions ultimately rests with media institutions and journalists and with audience members themselves. Journalists should approach comments as part of their overall ethical decision making, knowing that even with the best technology, comments are not a "set it and forget it" type of activity. Any flaw in a digital commenting system will be exploited by subversive actors. Journalists must move forward with digital discourse efforts knowing that members of the audience will impulsively post venomous and half-baked thoughts in comment sections.

A comment section can be compared to a car. A car is a handy conveyance tool, but can mutate into a deadly weapon depending on the actions of the driver. New drivers, especially, are unlikely to stop at an intersection unless there is a signal warning them to do so and consequences if they don't. The possibility of meaningful digital deliberation is influenced by choices made about the format and the governance of the online discussion space. Most existing online forum designs promote dysfunctional behaviors among discussion participants. And they do not offer any incentives for participants to seek compromise.

A study by Thomas B. Ksiazek examining the structure and organization of user comments across 20 news websites determined that specific policies regarding user registration, moderation of comments and reputation-management systems could spur more productive dialogue.[14] Another study by Scott Wright and John Street about the impact of design suggests good or bad online deliberation should be viewed as dependent upon design and choice rather than being a predetermined product of technology.[15]

As stressed-out digital news publishers have tried balancing open public participation and free speech with the web's acrimonious conversation culture, many have called "timeouts" on user comments to consider new approaches. *The Verge,*[16] *New Haven Independent,*[17] *Chicago Sun Times,*[18] *Las Vegas Review Journal,*[19] *National Catholic Reporter,*[20] *St. Louis Post-Dispatch*[21] and *The Sacramento Bee*[22] are among the small and large news sites that have paused commenting. Others news outlets such as *Bloomberg,*[23] *The Telegraph*[24] and *Columbia Journalism Review*[25] removed onsite public feedback forums as part of site redesigns. Brand new sites have chosen to launch without comments, too, including female-centric sites *The Establishment*[26] *and Broadly.*[27] When *Vox* launched in 2014 without online comments, editors explained that "flame wars" turn off readers.[28]

Through the years, news sites have also experimented with a variety of user experience (UX) designs, comment moderation and troll-deterrent techniques, efforts aimed at tempering the ongoing toxicity. Most comment sections employ community-dependent moderation systems in which users help flag comments they deem inappropriate (or disagree with). Bad actors and repeat offenders can be kicked off forums through banning or the more creative "ghost banning" in which blocked users can see their own commenting activity, but no one else can. "Disemvoweling" is a shaming technique where all vowels are removed from offensive postings, making them ridiculous and difficult to read.[29] The *Milwaukee Journal Sentinel* is one of several news sites that limit comment participation to only paying subscribers.[30] In February 2015, *Tablet* magazine began charging readers $2 to leave comments.[31]

Algorithms help to weed out inappropriate comments, but no computer logic has been developed yet that can't be gamed. Google and *The New York Times* are experimenting with artificial intelligence to "auto-moderate"

50% to 80% of the comments on *nytimes.com*.[32] Big news organizations such as *ESPN* and *The Washington Post* employ commercial third-party moderation to deal with the millions of comments their sites attract. While hiring human beings to screen and remove offensive comments in an effort to obtain better comments can be effective, moderation services are costly, and the work can be soul crushing.[33] Some sites that have switched to Facebook's commenting system give anecdotal evidence of slightly less toxic commentary, but Facebook's platform doesn't do anything to encourage thoughtful dialogue either, and the massive social network suffers from its own problems of fake news, violent videos, bullying and harassment.

Cleveland.com in December 2016 instituted a method editors call "pre-curation" to ensure comments are on-topic and maintain the Ohio news organization's requirements for civility. "Those who would poison such a conversation quickly realize they can't break through our moderation and go away," wrote *Advance Ohio* editor Chris Quinn. "Or—and I've seen this happen—they edit their thoughts to make them civil and join the conversation."[34]

In November 2015, the publishing platform Medium began allowing users to hide reader comments—called "responses"—acknowledging that "sometimes you may not want to get in a discussion."[35] The social video platform Periscope in May 2016 enabled an interesting abuse-reporting system in which "flash juries" of users judge the offensiveness of flagged comments.[36] And this novel comment approach in Norway may yet make its way to the United States: people who want to join discussions on the Norwegian news site *NRKbeta* must pass a three-question quiz to ensure comprehension of the connected news story before they can chime in with a comment.[37]

Deciding how a commenting system looks and operates are choices publishers can make with intent. These decisions affect the nature of readers' and moderators' experiences, as well as the quality and level of audience participation. Humans will mentally check out if they feel overwhelmed by too much information. The most common online comment layout found on news sites is a one-column thread below the news content, usually requiring a click to view, with the most recent or most up-voted comment appearing at the top. The most popular third-party comment systems used by news sites, such as Disqus, LiveFyre, Viafoura and Facebook, follow this one-column UX format. When the *Daily Dot* ended its on-site commenting in 2015, the editors cited frustration with the design of existing third-party comment systems as a reason for the shutdown. Other comment layouts have featured annotated comments, sidebar columns of comments, categorized comments such as "reader picks" and "editors' picks," as well as stand-alone discussion areas.

Judith Donath of Harvard University's Berkman Center pointed out in a 2017 Pew Research survey that the more socially complex question we need to solve is how to facilitate constructive discussions among people who disagree. "We need to rethink the structure of online discourse. The role of discussion host/moderator is poorly supported by current tech—and many discussions would proceed much better in a model other than the current linear free for all," Donath wrote. "Our face-to-face interactions have amazing subtlety—we can encourage or dissuade with slight changes in gaze, facial expression, etc. We need to create tools for conversation hosts . . . that help them to gracefully steer conversations."[38]

One online social interaction theory I stumbled upon during my research for this book compares the functionality and longevity of "plazas" versus "warrens."[39] The idea, described in an October 2010 blog post by Venkatesh Rao and attributed to Xianhang Zhang, posits that "plaza" architectures are large online environments centrally designed for general audiences, where participants get the biggest-picture view. But the openness and legibility of a plaza makes it brittle and difficult to maintain order, leading to eventual atrophy and decline. Open online comment sections are like plazas. Alternatively, "warrens" are narrow paths with barriers to entry. Since warrens are smaller and rely on cooperation, they are theoretically more resilient.[40] As many news sites have given up on their "plazas" of digital discussion, more have begun experimenting with "warrens" of discourse guided by journalist moderators.

For example, *The Washington Post* created a closed Slack group specifically for women to discuss the wage gap.[41] As part of *PBS NewsHour*'s 2016 election coverage, weekend anchor Hari Sreenivasan hosted a private Facebook group of engaged voters who were still evaluating the candidates.[42] A lively Facebook group has sprung up around the NPR series *Your Money and Your Life* with 30,000+ members, who discuss investment and personal finance decisions largely among themselves, with occasional input from NPR.[43] In December 2016, Spaceship Media, a startup built around a reporting model it calls "dialogue journalism," filled a closed Facebook group with 50 women, half of them Trump voters from Alabama and the other half from San Francisco, to do nothing more than talk.[44] The *Boston Globe* also started a private Facebook group in December 2016 for subscribers to discuss the news with each other and *Globe* staffers. The group is on the record but moderated, and foul language or personal attacks are not allowed.[45]

The relative success of these "warrens" demonstrates that discussions don't have to be convened on every news story by default. Journalists can work with the audience in "some degree of emergent collaboration"[46] to mindfully determine which topics merit more in-depth public conversation.

Infusing more civility and veracity into our digital deliberations is the selling point for newer audience engagement efforts by Civil Comments, the Coral Project and Hearken. Civil Comments requires users to rate the civility of several other comments on the news site—and then their own comment—before submission. It uses crowdsourced moderation and machine-learning algorithms to weed out trolls and spam and ensure higher quality comments without the heavy hands of moderators deleting offending posts.[47]

The Coral Project—a joint effort between *The New York Times*, *The Washington Post*, the Mozilla Foundation and the Knight Foundation— is developing a cache of free open-source applications any site can use to improve audience exchanges.[48] The Coral Project's Trust app, for example, aims to scale moderation of user comments by focusing on user contribution history.[49] Hearken is an audience-engagement initiative born of public radio that uses "questions as the new comments" by tapping into the crowd at the start of a newsgathering initiative instead of culling audience reactions at the end. Users are rarely involved *pre*-publication. Journalists are typically absent *post*-publication. Filling those gaps with engagement is a ripe opportunity for news purveyors.

Championing Good Conversations

> We have responsibility to think how to build systems that tend to produce constructive criticism and harmony, as opposed to negativity and bullying.
> —Web pioneer Tim Berners-Lee[50]

When I went back and read all those vitriolic comments about the 2008 Hartford hit-and-run during my research for this book, I was surprised how they didn't come across as abhorrent to me eight years later. At what point will our ongoing exposure to virulent online speech begin to normalize it?

Without a champion, the dark and ugly tone of online comments is not expected to brighten anytime soon. A 2017 survey of 1,500 digital experts by the Pew Research Center concluded that uncivil and manipulative behaviors on the internet will persist—and are likely to get worse—leading to the stark division of digital discourse into algorithm-patrolled, regulated "safe spaces" and chaotic, free-for-all zones. Many experts worry this will hurt the open exchange of ideas.[51]

Better awareness of how comments work, understanding the motivation of commenters and learning from the flaws in comment systems can help journalists debug their professional routines, conventions, culture and technology to better facilitate more meaningful online discourse while keeping the angry mobs, trolls, spammers, bots and propagandists at bay.

Clearly not all digital "conversation" qualifies as "deliberation." Discussions in news site forums and on social media are unlikely to follow the high ideals set for deliberative democracy. "Speech is not always so rational, tolerance toward those who hold opposing views is at times wanting, and the forms of interaction are not always so civil," Peter Dahlgren observed. Although this exploration of journalism and online comments catalogued the many problems surrounding public digital discourse, it is not an argument against online comments, online free speech or online anonymity. Aristotle wrote, "virtue is a mean state between extremes."[52] For every virtue suggested by the ancient Greek philosopher, there are corresponding vices of deficiency and excess. Journalists risk going overboard by eliminating public debate about difficult topics or failing to host and moderate discussions, by enforcing a narrow view of "civility," silencing alternative voices or excluding points of view.

"In my view, the worst places to visit aren't the comment jungles of 4chan or YouTube, but the overly manicured comment lawns of some newspapers," wrote journalist Michael Erard.[53] Mainstream news organizations shouldn't be trying to put a lid on commenting culture's excesses, Erard argued, but rethinking the relationship between creators and commenters in more fundamental ways.

Let's ruminate on the question of who is worse for our digital democracy—a lurker or a troll? As a journalist, I'd argue that both are equally detrimental, especially if the lurker is a professional news organization that doesn't intervene to limit the damage caused by trolls. What the modern practice of journalism in the digital space requires is not more bystander apathy or extreme policing but action in recognizing commenters as democratic actors fighting for what they believe, even when they come dressed as trolls. Finding new ways to get people to listen and find consensus are key to improving the caustic news comment environment.

Roxanne Starr Hiltz, Murray Turoff and Suzanne Keller in the 1994 book *The Network Nation: Human Communication via Computer*, wrote:

> For most forms of communication, societies have had decades or even centuries to develop cultural guidelines for appropriate use. These are enforced as norms, taught to children by their parents, and embodied in codes of law. There has not been time, however, for an adequate ethical and legal framework to emerge to regulate the use of [computer-mediated communication]. Lacking this, groups must explicitly

formulate policies and socialize new members about appropriate and inappropriate behavior.[54]

Journalism has the imperative to create digital spaces where respectful disagreement and discussion are possible. Meaningful public discourse will require news outlets to "be the aggressor"—the driving force in convening conversations.[55] That will require the consistent application of journalistic rigor to what news purveyors discover, collect and amplify online. It means organizing information for maximum understanding, keeping conversations on point, correcting errors, debunking misinformation, seeking out diverse participants, including varied perspectives, and adding value to citizens' comments above the reactive social media layer.

"Take a step back and look at . . . how fragmented our conversations have become. How scary they've become. How fast information and mis-information is shaped to serve the reality people want, instead of the reality that is," observed Amanda Zamora. "By abandoning comments, news organizations are not only giving up an important role in shaping public discourse—they're giving up a key avenue toward having direct, sustainable relationships with their audiences. Those relationships are vital to any future we have in this business."[56]

Public digital discourse is a crucial component of democracy—one that journalists and news organizations must stop treating with indifference or detachment. People do not always agree or argue in a civilized way. Freedom of expression on an open internet means more communication, which means more conflict. Online comments are conflict.

If journalists truly value the role they play in democracy, then news organizations large and small need to make thoughtful investments in the public discourse of today, happening online. There are possibilities *within* the conflict of comments.

Notes

1. Esmail, Sam. "Eps1.2_d3bug.mkv." Mr. Robot. USA Network. 8 Jul. 2015. Television.
2. Rubin, Thomas C. "Facebook, Stand Up or Get Out." *Re/Code*. 31 May 2016. Web. www.recode.net/2016/5/31/11821868/facebook-thune-thiel-gawker-congress-first-amendment
3. Jankowski, N., & M. van Selm. "Traditional News Media Online: An Examination of Added Value." *Television News Research: Recent European Approaches and Findings*. Berlin: Quintessence Publishing Co., 2001. 375–92. Print.
4. Kovach, Bill, and Tom Rosenstiel. The *Elements of Journalism: What Newspeople Should Know and the Public Should Expect*. New York: Three Rivers, 2007. Print.

5. Silverman, Craig. "This Analysis Shows How Viral Fake Election News Stories Outperformed Real News on Facebook." *BuzzFeed*. 16 Nov. 2016. Web. www. buzzfeed.com/craigsilverman/viral-fake-election-news-outperformed-real-news-on-facebook

6. U.S. President Donald J. Trump's personal Twitter account: https://twitter.com/realdonaldtrump

7. Fishkin, James S. *When the People Speak: Deliberative Democracy and Public Consultation*. Oxford; New York: Oxford University Press, 2009. 103. Print.

8. Sillisen, Lene Bech, Chris Ip, and David Uberti. "Journalism and the Power of Emotions." *Columbia Journalism Review*. May–Jun. 2015. Web. www.cjr.org/analysis/journalism_and_the_power_of_emotions.php

9. FitzGerald, Tucker. "Intolerant Liberals." *Medium*. 2 Feb. 2017. Web. https://medium.com/@tuckerfitzgerald/intolerant-liberals-4ecd712ac939

10. Sunstein, Cass R. "Democracy and Filtering." Communications of the ACM—The Blogosphere. ACM 47, Dec. 2004. 12, 57–59. Web. http://dx.doi.org/10.1145/1035134.1035166

11. Rosenstiel, Tom. "News as Collaborative Intelligence: Correcting the Myths about News in the Digital Age." *The Brookings Institute*. 30 Jun. 2015. Web. www.brookings.edu/research/papers/2015/06/30-collaborative-intelligence-myths-digital-age-rosenstiel

12. Gere, Charlie. "Introduction." *Digital Culture*. 2nd Edition. London: Reaktion Books, 2009. Web. via Google Books. https://books.google.com/books?id=d9Xlw AXSoDcC&pg=PT13

13. Joyce, Michael. "There Will Be Trolls." *North Coast Journal*. 1 Dec. 2016. Web. www.northcoastjournal.com/humboldt/there-will-be-trolls/Content?oid=4191499

14. Ksiazek, Thomas B. "Civil Interactivity: How News Organizations' Commenting Policies Explain Civility and Hostility in User Comments." *Journal of Broadcasting & Electronic Media*. Nov. 2015. Volume 59, Issue 4. 556–73. Web. www.tandfonline.com/doi/abs/10.1080/08838151.2015.1093487

15. Wright, Scott, and John Street. "Democracy, Deliberation and Design: The Case of Online Discussion Forums." *New Media & Society*. Oct. 2007. Volume 9, Issue 5. 849–69. Web. http://journals.sagepub.com/doi/abs/10.1177/1461444807 081230

16. Patel, Nilay. "We're Turning Comments Off for a Bit." *The Verge*. 6 Jul. 2015. Web. www.theverge.com/2015/7/6/8901115/were-turning-comments-off-for-a-bit

17. Bass, Paul. "Time Out!" *New Haven Independent*. 7 Feb. 2012. Web. www.newhavenindependent.org/index.php/archives/entry/time_out/

18. Kirkland, Sam. "Sun-Times Kills Comments Until It Can Fix 'Morass of Negativity, Racism, and Hate Speech'." *Poynter Institute*. 12 Apr. 2014. Web. www.poynter.org/2014/sun-times-kills-comments-until-it-can-fix-morass-of-negativity-racism-and-hate-speech/247525/

19. "Why We Restored Our Comment Boards Today." *Las Vegas Review Journal*. 5 Feb. 2015. Web. medium.com/@reviewjournal/why-we-restored-our-comment-boards-today-215b5f740003

20. Cohen, Pam. "Before Comments Are Reinstated, Verify Your Email Address." *National Catholic Reporter*. 10 Feb. 2014. Web. www.ncronline.org/blogs/ncr-today/comments-are-reinstated-verify-your-email-address

21. "Editorial: No Comments: An Experiment in Elevating the Conversation." *St. Louis Post Dispatch.* 8 Dec. 2014. Web. http://webcache.googleusercontent. com/search?q=cache:www.stltoday.com/news/opinion/columns/the-platform/ article_072cf5a8-17fe-53ba-95fb-b945fbbde8ed.html

22. Terhaar, Janet. "The Bee Launches Improved Commenting Online." *Sacramento Bee.* 28 Mar. 2015. Web. www.sacbee.com/opinion/opn-columns-blogs/ joyce-terhaar/article16346735.html

23. Sweney, Mark, and Frances Perraudin. "Bloomberg Switches Off Comments in Website Redesign." *The Guardian.* 28 Jan. 2015. Web. www.theguardian.com/ media/2015/jan/28/bloomberg-switches-off-comments-in-website-redesign

24. Sweney, Mark. "Telegraph Suspends Comment on Relaunched Online Content." *The Guardian.* 22 Feb. 2016. Web. www.theguardian.com/media/2016/ feb/22/telegraph-suspends-comment-relaunched-online-content

25. Murtha, Jack. "How Audience Engagement Editors Are Guiding Online Discussions." *Columbia Journalism Review.* 15 Sept. 2015. Web. www.cjr.org/ analysis/before_many_americans_had_awoken.php

26. Oluo, Ijeoma. "Why We Don't Have Comments." *The Establishment.* 19 Nov. 2015. Web. https://theestablishment.co/why-we-dont-have-a-comments-section-4b491cc4fab

27. Lanz, Michelle. "Broadly: Vice's New Women-Centric Site Nixes the Comment Section to Avoid Trolls." *The Frame.* Southern California Public Radio. 6 Aug. 2015. Web. www.scpr.org/programs/the-frame/2015/08/06/44011/broadly-vices-new-women-centric-site-nixes-the-com/

28. Bell, Melissa. "Three Weeks of Vox." *Vox.com.* 28 Apr. 2014. Web. www.vox. com/2014/4/28/5659728/three-weeks-of-vox-tell-us-what-you-think

29. Hamilton, Anita. "Best Inventions of 2008: 42. Disemvoweling." *Time.com.* 29 Oct. 2008. Web. http://content.time.com/time/specials/packages/article/0,28 804,1852747_1854195_1854185,00.html

30. Stanley, George. "JSOnline Forums Will Be Limited to Paid Subscribers." *Journal Sentinel.* 6 Feb. 2016. Web. www.jsonline.com/news/faq-what-you-need-to-know-about-jsonlines-commenting-changes-b99664500z1-367890961.html

31. O'Donovan, Caroline. "Troll Toll: Tablet Is Now Charging Its Readers for the Right to Comment." *Nieman Lab.* 10 Feb. 2015. Web. www.niemanlab.org/2015/ 02/troll-toll-tablet-is-now-charging-its-readers-for-the-right-to-comment/

32. Auerbach, David. "If Only AI Could Save Us from Ourselves." *MIT Technology Review.* 13 Dec. 2016. Web. www.technologyreview.com/s/603072/if-only-ai-could-save-us-from-ourselves/

33. Chen, Adrian. "The Laborers Who Keep Dick Pics and Beheadings Out of Your Facebook Feed." *Wired.* 23 Oct. 2014. Web. www.wired.com/2014/10/ content-moderation/

34. Quinn, Chris. "Have We Tapped into a Solution for Online Comments and Robust Civic Discourse?" *Cleveland.com.* 15 Dec. 2016. Web. www.cleveland. com/opinion/index.ssf/2016/12/might_we_have_a_potential_solu.html

35. Reader, Ruth. "Medium Now Lets Users Shield Themselves from Nasty Comments." *VentureBeat.* 5 Nov. 2015. Web. https://venturebeat.com/2015/11/05/ medium-now-lets-users-shield-themselves-from-nasty-comments/

36. Wagner, Kurt. "Periscope Has a New Plan to Fight Back against Internet Trolls." *Re/code.* 31 May 2016. Web. www.recode.net/2016/5/31/11803070/periscope-abuse-safety-update-internet-trolls

37. Lichterman, Joseph. "This Site Is 'Taking the Edge Off Rant Mode' by Making Readers Pass a Quiz before Commenting." *Nieman Lab.* 1 Mar. 2017. Web. www.niemanlab.org/2017/03/this-site-is-taking-the-edge-off-rant-mode-by-making-readers-pass-a-quiz-before-commenting/

38. Donath, Judith, as quoted by Lee Rainie, Janna Anderson, and Jonathan Albright. "The Future of Free Speech, Trolls, Anonymity and Fake News Online." *Pew Research Center.* 29 Mar. 2017. Web. www.pewinternet.org/2017/03/29/the-future-of-free-speech-trolls-anonymity-and-fake-news-online

39. Rao, Venkatesh. "Warrens, Plazas and the Edge of Legibility." *Ribbonfarm Blog.* 27 Oct. 2010. Web. www.ribbonfarm.com/2010/10/27/warrens-plazas-and-the-edge-of-legibility/

40. Ibid.

41. Bilton, Ricardo. "The Washington Post Is Using Slack to Create a Reader Community Focused on the Gender Pay Gap." *Nieman Lab.* 30 Jun. 2016. Web. www.niemanlab.org/2016/06/the-washington-post-is-using-slack-to-create-a-reader-community-focused-on-the-gender-pay-gap/

42. Cohen, David. "Facebook Group Plays Role in PBS NewsHour's Democratic Debate Coverage." *Adweek.* 11 Feb. 2016. Web. www.adweek.com/digital/facebook-group-pbs-newshour-democratic-debate-021116/

43. NPR's "Your Money, Your Life." Facebook Group. Web. www.facebook.com/groups/yourmoneyandlife/

44. Jeremy, Hay, and Eve Pearlman. "As Conversation Winds Down, Women from Alabama and California Discuss Race, Other Challenges." *Al.com.* 15 Jan. 2017. Web.www.al.com/news/birmingham/index.ssf/2017/01/as_conversation_winds_down_wom.html

45. Wang, Shan. "With Its Subscribers Facebook Group, the Boston Globe Is Mining the Stickiest Corners of the Platform." *Nieman Lab.* 6 Jan. 2017. Web. www.niemanlab.org/2017/01/with-its-subscribers-facebook-group-the-boston-globe-is-mining-the-stickiest-corners-of-the-platform/

46. Rao. "Warrens, Plazas and the Edge of Legibility."

47. Schneider, Daniel J., and Eric Lubbers. "Our Article Comments Have been a Cesspool of Trolls and Spam for Years: Enter Civil Comments." *Denver Post.* 22 May 2017. Web. www.denverpost.com/2017/05/22/denver-post-civil-comments/

48. Farhi, Paul. "Washington Post, New York Times and Mozilla Team up for New Web Site Comment System." *Washington Post.* 19 Jun. 2014. Web. www.washingtonpost.com/lifestyle/style/washington-post-new-york-times-and-mozilla-team-up-for-new-web-site-comment-system/2014/06/19/fa836e90-f71e-11e3-8aa9-dad2ec039789_story.html

49. Lichterman, Joseph. "The Coral Project Unveils Its First Product to Make Comments Better." *Nieman Lab.* 15 Mar. 2016. Web. www.niemanlab.org/2016/03/the-coral-project-unveils-its-first-product-to-make-comments-better/

50. Gothard, Peter. "Tim Berners-Lee Slams Twitter's 'Negativity and Bullying'; Suggests New 'Constructive' Social Networks Now Required." *computing.co.uk.* 1 Feb. 2016. Web. www.computing.co.uk/ctg/news/2444382/tim-berners-lee-slams-twitter-s-negativity-and-bullying-suggests-new-contructive-social-networks-now-required

51. Rainie, Lee, Janna Anderson, and Jonathan Albright. "The Future of Free Speech, Trolls, Anonymity and Fake News Online." *Pew Research Center.* 29 Mar.

2017. Web. www.pewinternet.org/2017/03/29/the-future-of-free-speech-trolls-anonymity-and-fake-news-online

52. Aristotle. "Virtue as the Mean between Two Extreme States." *Nicomachean Ethics Book II*. Translated by W. D. Ross. Web. http://web.mnstate.edu/gracyk/courses/web%20publishing/AristotleVirtueAsMean.htm

53. Erard, Michael. "No Comments." *New York Times*. 20 Sept. 2013. Web. www.nytimes.com/2013/09/22/magazine/no-comments.html?pagewanted=all&_r=0

54. Hiltz, Roxanne Starr, Murray Turoff, and Keller Suzanne. *The Network Nation: Human Communication via Computer*. Cambridge, MA: MIT, 1994. Print.

55. Jurkowitz, Mark. "Creating Community-Centered, Not Candidate-Centered, Narratives." *Nieman Reports*. 18 Nov. 2016. Web. http://niemanreports.org/articles/creating-community-centered-not-candidate-centered-narratives/

56. Zamora, Amanda. "Comments Are Changing: Our Commitment to Audiences Shouldn't." *The Poynter Institute*. 31 Aug. 2016. Web. www.poynter.org/2016/comments-are-changing-our-commitment-to-audiences-shouldnt/428399/

Index

For Product Safety Concerns and Information please contact our EU
representative GPSR@taylorandfrancis.com
Taylor & Francis Verlag GmbH, Kaufingerstraße 24, 80331 München, Germany